ENVIRONMENT AND SUSTAINABILITY POLICY

A real strength of Stephen Dovers' book is that it starts with a clear acknowledgement of the challenges, in policy and action terms, of the current transition we are just beginning; a transition from managing environmental effects to the much more complex goal of developing more sustainable ways of meeting society's needs and wants. Against this canvas he unpicks our current policy processes and finds them inadequate for the advancing environmental sustainability.

Stephen Dovers' list of what would constitute a "credible commitment" to sustainability in terms of believable reforms should be compulsory reading for all local and central government politicians.

Dr J Morgan Williams
Parliamentary Commissioner for the Environment, New Zealand

... a seminal contribution to the literature on learning for sustainability, a truly comprehensive analysis of the issues and policy implications. It is not a toolkit but discusses all major challenges of the integration of social, economic and ecological issues under various perspectives. Dovers' insights on participation, integration and institutional change in particular will be welcomed by educators and policy professionals, students, change managers and administrators at the cutting edge of sustainability.

Adjunct Professor Paul J Perkins
Chair, National Environmental and Education Council, Australia

Sustainability is the pivot around which global environmental policy making is supposed to revolve. Yet the concept is often poorly understood, and its translation into domestic policy and firm action suffers from confusion about whether sustainability is merely aspirational window dressing or a serious goal of public administration. In this valuable and thoughtful book, Stephen Dovers encapsulates what is going wrong in the translation process, from strategic policy setting to implementation and evaluation of decision-making; and offers a valuable framework for improving our understanding of how integrated, participatory and accountable processes can deliver on the good intent but weak commitment that has to date marked much of environmental decision-making in Australia.

Professor Gerry Bates
Environmental Law and Policy Consultant

The complexity of ecological sustainability demands new approaches to the formulation and evaluation of environmental policy and practice – Stephen Dovers' *Environment and Sustainability Policy* provides an important and timely framework to help with this critically important task.

Dovers masterfully explains why researchers, land managers, and environmental professionals are all deeply enmeshed in government policy making and how all these different players can work more effectively together to achieve environmental sustainability. This book is essential reading for anyone involved in Natural Resource Management.

Professor David Bowman
Director of Australian Research Council
Key Centre for Tropical Wildlife Management,
Charles Darwin University

ENVIRONMENT AND SUSTAINABILITY POLICY

Creation·Implementation·Evaluation

Stephen Dovers

THE FEDERATION PRESS
2005

Published in Sydney by:
    The Federation Press
    PO Box 45, Annandale, NSW, 2038
    71 John St, Leichhardt, NSW, 2040
    Ph (02) 9552 2200 Fax (02) 9552 1681.
    E-mail: info@federationpress.com.au
    Website: http://www.federationpress.com.au

National Library of Australia
Cataloguing-in-Publication entry

    Dovers, Stephen.
    Environment and sustainability policy:
    creation, implementation, evaluation.

    Bibliography.
    Includes index.
    ISBN 1 86287 540 5

    1. Sustainable development. 2. Environmental policy. I. Title.

338.927

Typeset in Palatino Linotype (text) and Trebuchet MS (headings)
    by The Federation Press, Sydney.
Printed by Southwood Press Pty Ltd, Sydney
    on Cyclus 100% recycled paper.

Preface

WHY THIS BOOK?

This book seeks to provide a basis for analysing and prescribing public policy and institutional responses to further the social goals of protecting the environment and the more complex and profound goal of sustainability. It does so in response to experiences over the past two decades of research on and involvement in policy processes which have emphasised four issues.

The first is that, by and large, current policy responses to sustainability, and even to more narrowly defined and specific environmental problems, are inadequate. That is not simply an isolated judgment but the widely echoed view of stakeholders and even of collective governments at forums such as the 2002 World Summit on Sustainable Development. The phenomena of policy *ad hocery* and amnesia – uncoordinated efforts and a lack of accrued understanding and capacity – are easily enough identified. The second issue is that it should be more evident than is apparent that environment is not an easy policy arena and the larger sustainability agenda represents a particularly difficult set of policy and institutional challenges. Effective policy and institutional reform to address the higher order social goal of sustainability is a generational task, yet there is too often an expectation of quick policy gratification. Policy changes over the past decade or so have been mostly superficial, not extending to the institutional arrangements that in contemporary society determine the systemic causes of sustainability problems.

The third issue relates to the relative novelty of sustainability and even better known environmental issues – we are simply not that skilled at addressing these yet. There is not a coherent policy field, with matching policy processes and institutional settings and the necessary human resources and knowledge to run them effectively. That leads to the fourth issue: "policy" is clearly an important concept and reality, yet is subject to highly varied understanding amongst those concerned with environment and sustainability. This retards progress. To some "policy" is shorthand for a complex phenomenon that requires specialist understanding, for others it is something about which any one opinion is as valid as any other. For others again policy is a mystery, or an everyday term used interchangeably with laws, organisations, institutions and politics. For some in government, the term means a glossy document or well-fashioned public statement and not much before or afterward. A better common understanding of policy would be a useful thing, and that is one aim here.

In response, this book presents an approach to environmental and sustainability policy meant to be simple and accessible enough to be *used*, but detailed enough to be *useful*. It seeks to combine an appreciation of natural-human system interdependencies and sustainability problems, with an appreciation of the contributions of the traditional policy-oriented disciplines. These disciplines often fail to gain purchase on sustainability problems, but offer significant insights.

The organising structure for the book is a framework (*not* a model) of the elements of a "good" policy process – defined as being comprehensive, purposeful, open and informed. While any analytical or prescriptive framework is unavoidably an arbitrary construct, it is hoped that at least the book is more useable as a result of using such a clear structuring device.

The first part of the book frames the area of concern – the policy domain of environment and sustainability – in a manner that: (a) invites purposeful problem-solving (rather than simply debate over issues); (b) surveys key ideas about policy processes; and (c) presents the analytical and prescriptive framework. The second part works through the framework, with sequential chapters describing the challenges of framing problems and policies, policy implementation, monitoring and evaluation, and participation and accountability. The third part deals with key challenges in environment and sustainability: policy coordination and integration, and institutional change.

The book does not recommend specific policy outcomes or instruments, but is about the *processes* through which these can be selected. Official policy rhetoric about sustainability already paints a future which is not being properly pursued, so this author does not need to dwell on what specific outcomes would equal sustainability: closer rather than further away will suffice. Good policy products may emerge accidentally from poor process, but we will not know why and therefore be unable to learn from the "experiment". That is a key theme here. We do not know much about how to advance sustainability through policy and institutional reform, and are attempting or promising to do so in the face of complexity and uncertainty. That instructs us to view all institutional, policy and on-ground management changes as experiments, to be watched, adjusted and persisted with. This book seeks to improve our ability to construct and undertake such experiments.

In line with the intention to keep the book as short as possible, detailed case studies are not provided. Rather, illustrative examples are used to convey the key arguments and to show the applicability of the frameworks and checklists. This book is not a public policy text, of which there are many (and some will be recommended), but rather it draws on ideas from public policy and elsewhere and applies those to environment and sustainability. Similarly, detailed literature reviews are not provided, but rather sufficient references and sources to provide an entry to greater detail.

Stephen Dovers
Queanbeyan, NSW
April 2005

CONTENTS

LIST OF FIGURES AND TABLES

Figures

Tables

ACKNOWLEDGEMENTS

This book grows out of a body of work carried out by myself and various colleagues over a decade and a half. It is meant to help our policy communities – people and groups within and outside of government – to better address the modern challenge of creating a more ecologically sustainable and humanly desirable state of affairs.

While I am at fault for any weaknesses or oversights, whatever strengths and utility are in the following pages can likely be traced to others. The Centre for Resource and Environmental Studies at The Australian National University has been a superb base for such work. Bob Wasson encouraged this particular venture. Various colleagues over a long period have helped me formulate ideas, including Robin Connor, Stephen Boyden, Richard Price, John Handmer, Hezri Adnan, Catherine Mobbs, Richard Baker, Mick Common, Tony Norton, Su Wild River, Jon Barnett, Heidi Ellemor, Libby Robin, David Lindenmayer, Ian White, Alice Roughley, Andrew Campbell, Richard Baker, Simon Marsden, Rosemary James, David Stern, Brett Odgers, Jann Williams and Rob Dyball. And others who I have overlooked to mention, such as the participants in projects such as "ANU 17". I have worked and published formally with some of these, but owe just as much to numerous unreported interactions. Land & Water Australia supported key related research projects.

Structuring a book around a policy framework is not unusual in public policy, and the immediate inspiration for doing so here comes from Bridgman and Davis' (2001) very useful and admirably short text, *The Australian Policy Handbook*. Whether the quite different framework and discussion in this volume works as well as theirs does is another question. I am happy that Margaret Farmer and Chris Holt at Federation Press took this book on, and hope it is useful enough to sufficient readers to make them happy as well. To Michele, Stuart and Emma, thanks for the support and tolerance. Sorry for the lack of more interesting collective activities while this was being written.

PART I

POLICY AND THE ENVIRONMENT

Chapter 1

ORIENTATION AND INTRODUCTION

This chapter introduces environment and sustainability and describes the logic of the book. It deals with the nature of policy problems in environment and sustainability, and the policy and institutional challenges that make up the modern sustainability agenda. It notes the general inadequacy of policy responses thus far, and the magnitude of the task of moving towards sustainability. It then considers the role of policy knowledge and learning, and sets out the definitions of the core terms and concepts used in later chapters. Finally, it explains the organisation and structure of the book and the approach taken to providing references and sources of further reading.

Environment or sustainability: Implications

> [T]here is nothing more difficult to carry out, nor more doubtful of success, nor more dangerous to handle, than to initiate a new order of things (Machiavelli 1940 (1532): 21).

Over recent decades it has become apparent that the pathway of human development is in many ways ecologically unsustainable and humanly undesirable. The severity of the "sustainability problem" is contested, but at the same time as environmental and human degradation continue (despite much rhetoric and some action) it appears that the trend is one of greater evidence and concern, not less. Three landmark international meetings on the environment have occurred in recent decades: the first in Stockholm in 1972, the unprecedented United Nations Conference on Environment and Development (UNCED) in Rio de Janeiro in 1992, and the World Summit on Sustainable Development (WSSD) in Johannesburg in 2002. Each time, the problems recognised have been more complex, the urgency greater, the weight of evidence stronger, and the debate about what to do louder. What has been most consistent is the recognition that significant policy and institutional change was required, but not enough had been done so far.

1960's Start of Movement

Our understanding of the nature of the problems has changed considerably over that time. The first wave of modern environmental concern, from the 1960s, and policy responses to it, was largely about a suite of separate issues that could be treated reactively, with ameliorative or "end-of-pipe" treatments. Environmental protection (pollution control), straightforward approaches to nature conservation (reserving a few areas of land and species), and limiting some resource extraction, were the main responses. Over time, the fact that causes rather than symptoms of environmental problems had to be addressed became more apparent – for example, reducing consumption or waste production rather than simply cleaning up or controlling the environmental damage, or managing biodiversity across landscapes as opposed to simply reserving a few bits. Allied to this, it became obvious that "environmental" problems were, in fact, social and economic challenges, as it is societies and economies – individual and collective human behaviours – that cause the problems, not the environment itself. Combined with rising concern over poverty and human development, this drove the transition from a purely "environmental debate" to the more recent *sustainability* debate which seeks to integrate environmental, social and economic dimensions.

This book reflects that transition in that it is about narrower environmental concerns and policy, but also about the quite different agenda of sustainability. It does so for two reasons. First, because that is where I perceive most societies and policy processes are presently located: still struggling with more familiar environmental issues while only beginning to comprehend and respond to the recent emergence of sustainability ideas. Second, because separate environmental problems and policy responses to them are still as important, if not more so than ever, even as we try and translate our understanding and policy responses to the larger sustainability agenda.

Continuing to deal with separate environmental problems while at the same time attempting to integrate these across landscapes, catchments, regions and nations, *and* seriously attending the sustainability challenge, suggests a much bigger effort than is currently being mounted. Long-term sustainability problems beg collective responses. This suggests that governments or other collective institutions must be central, yet this is problematic given recent and current political trends that discount the value of government coordination and collective efforts in favour of

4

individual and market approaches. The sorts of comprehensive, long-term policy processes described in this book run against that trend.

So it is unlikely that, in the near term at least, the sort of thorough policy efforts set out in the following chapters will be made. If governments and other parts of society cannot or will not commit the necessary resources, patience and will to improving policy and institutional capacities for sustainability, then the limits of what is being done should be clearly recognised, so that false expectations of policy completeness can be avoided. That way, policy initiatives can be understood as "experiments" in the face of complexity and uncertainty, and the prospects for learning and improvement left open.

How green is this book: Process versus product

Many writings on environmental policy and the challenge of sustainability advocate specific policy positions or policy instruments, and/or policy outcomes in the form of different environmental or human conditions. These are the *products* of policy systems. This book does not do that, but is concerned with the *processes* through which environmental and sustainability policies, and henceforth actual outcomes, are considered and emerge. It is my view that policy processes have received less attention than they should have, and that this has retarded the achievement of policy and actual environmental change.

Like anyone, I have my own views about how environmental and human conditions should change, but these views will be suppressed as much as possible. That way, the book can concentrate on the processes through which a wide range of beliefs and positions, along with scientific and other knowledge, can be considered, debated and incorporated into durable policies. While advocacy of specific positions is the stuff of policy and politics, the purpose of this book is not to advance a position, but to assist three sets of people:

- Those who have a position to advocate, and how and where it might be presented;
- Those whose role in society, such as in government, is to make sense of many different positions; and

- Those who are concerned yet uncertain about environmental and sustainability issues and wish to learn more
  about both the substance of the issues and about how they
  can best be understood and addresses.

Policy processes are where these three sets of people can constructively interact. A concentration on process over product may
disappoint those who believe that significant and urgent improvement in environmental and human conditions are required.
However, such a belief is not as radical as it sounds, as official
policy statements at national and especially international levels
(for example, at UNCED in 1992 and the WSSD in 2002) contain
visions of a future that, while not revolutionary, certainly would be
significant departures from the current state of affairs. They also
set out objectives and guiding principles such as precaution and
policy integration that societies do not follow very well. These
statements are often vague and their implementation has been
widely recognised as insufficient, but they provide a vision that
says that society perceives a problem and knows the *general
direction* to follow. However, the *degree* of change required is open
to question, and differing opinions on that are currently being
contested through policy processes that are not very suitable to the
task. It is clear enough that the degree of change to believably
pursue sustainability may or may not be profound, but is certainly
significant and not trivial (eg, Bodkin & Keller 2004; Harris 2004).
That is enough for the purpose of this book.

Reflecting on the relationship between policy, science, politics
and community for the environment, Lee (1993) described politics
as "bounded conflict". Better policy processes can "bound" debate,
not in the sense of deleting outlying opinions, but rather in terms
of enabling and utilising different opinions and information
towards achieving more widely understood and durable policies.
Good policy products may somehow emerge from a poor process
but we will not know how. Good policy processes may well
produce policy failures – indeed that it quite likely in a complex
and uncertain field such as sustainability. But our ability to understand the reasons for failure will be enhanced and so will our
ability to learn and improve.

Policy targets explored:
Environment and sustainability

While environment and sustainability issues are important and highly topical, there is a great deal of uncertainty associated with them. Also, they are long-term problems and the sustainability agenda has only been properly recognised in the last two decades. This all means that societies are as yet unsure of the actual severity and implications of the problems, the most important causes, the best policy responses to undertake, and the most suitable institutional arrangements through which to mount these responses. As well, the problems have arisen from human behaviours and actions (and lack of actions) over decades and even centuries, and this requires careful assessment of past policy efforts to contribute to learning better responses. Thus the matter of improving underlying policy processes is hugely important, as the only certainty is that we will be evolving our understanding and policies for decades to come, and thus need persistence and purpose as well as flexibility over time.

So far, the term "sustainability" has not been defined, and the difference between it and "environmental" has not been clarified. Sustainability refers to the ability of human society to persist in the long term in a manner that satisfies human development demands but without threatening the integrity of the natural world. That is a distant goal, or a basic property of human systems, that will never be reached, as uncertainty will always be present and both social and environmental systems will change. The term "sustainable development" is more often used, and the standard definition is that in the landmark report *Our Common Future* of the World Commission on Environment and Development (WCED 1987: 43):

> Sustainable development is development which meets the needs of the present without compromising the ability of future generations to meet their own needs. It contains within it two key concepts:
>
> - the concept of 'needs', in particular the essential needs of the world's poor, to which overriding priority should be given; and
> - the idea of limitations imposed by the state of technology and social organization on the environment's ability to meet present and future needs.

Even the narrow notion of physical sustainability implies a concern for social equity between generations, a concern that must logically be extended to equity within each generation.

Such definitions are by their nature vague, and Chapters 3 and 6 discuss this in more depth. While the WCED definition is strongly human-centred, both its report and subsequent international expressions also give emphasis to the inherent value of nature. It is important to recognise the complexity of the sustainability idea, and Table 1.1 sets out the broad categories of issues that make up the sustainability agenda. Table 1.1 shows a suite of issues that are captured under the broad heading of sustainability and that are interrelated, but that can also be decomposed into subsets and specifics (see further Chapter 5).

The hallmark of the sustainability idea is the inclusion of issues in categories 3 and 4 (ecological life support services and human development) in the same problem set as traditional resource and environmental issues. The greatest achievement of the WCED was to push a move in thinking from environmental *versus* development, to environment *and* development. While that move is occurring, the process has a long way to go in terms of both understanding and policy change.

If we consider sustainability as a more abstract, possible state, then sustainable development becomes the term we have adopted to summarise the messy, contested process on moving toward that state. What must be recognised is that, in this sense, sustainability is not a simple or achievable goal and sustainable development not a near-term policy challenge. Harrison (1992) described sustainable development as the universally agreed goal of human progress, and if we look carefully at the agenda of issues in Table 1.1, or at the challenges set out in the foundational United Nations Rio Declaration of 1992 (see Chapter 3), then that claim is not too grand. Using the term sustainability to include both the end and the means, and taking it at its broadest, we can understand it as a *higher order social goal*, similar to other widely supported goals like democracy, equity, public health or justice. Such goals are not achieved quickly or simply. Thus, sustainability is a generational task, to be pursued persistently over many decades and through concerted learning and policy and institutional change (Connor and Dovers 2004).

Seeing sustainability as a higher order, long-term social goal invites both pessimistic and optimistic reactions. First, it shows the

Table 1.1: Constituent issues of sustainability

Issues	
1. Resource depletion and degradation	Loss of biological/genetic diversity (in wild species and ecosystems, and in domesticated species) Land resources, especially soils Water resources (quantity) Forests and timber resources Energy resources Mineral resources Fisheries Scenic and cultural amenity
2. Pollution and wastes	Atmospheric pollution (indoor and outdoor) Marine pollution Pollution of inland waters
3. Fundamental ecological life support services	Ecosystem integrity and evolutionary potential Nutrient cycles Climate change and associated effects
4. Society and the human condition	Population growth Economic development and poverty Food security Shelter Health and disease Rapid urbanisation Human rights and environmental justice Lack of skills, education and empowerment Debt and trade inequities

challenges to be very hard ones that will take a great deal of effort and time. But it also indicates that we should not expect rapid achievements, and that what has been achieved in the few years since the challenge was first defined can be viewed as understandably limited. After all, other higher order social goals such as democracy or justice are still being argued about and pursued, centuries after they emerged, even though in modern societies they have far more substantial institutional and policy underpinnings than the goal of sustainability has.

At present, policy and institutional settings and the information and human resources that make these work are underdeveloped in the sustainability domain. Given the recent and complex nature of the problems, that is both something that can reasonably be expected, and something that requires significant effort. A stronger conceptualisation of environment and sustainability as a problem set confronting policy processes and a more adequate set of frameworks and tools for policy-making are part of that effort, and the intended contribution of this book. Environmental policy research was portrayed by Walker (1992: 253) thus:

> [T]hough there are no established methodologies either for policy analysis ex post facto or for evaluation of proposed policies, there does exist a grab-bag of useful perspectives and techniques, analytical and evaluative. The practice of environmental policy studies will undoubtedly, over time, lead to their refinement. Eventually, there may emerge approaches with broad acceptance and proven efficacy.

There is no reason to differ with this opinion more than a decade later, although much progress has been made. Environmental policy research is still evolving, and so too is environmental policy practice. Too often, efforts in the environment and sustainability domain are characterised by "policy ad hocery and amnesia" – unconnected, partial policy interventions, that are poorly implemented and monitored, and thus neither work as well as they might or contribute to ongoing policy improvement. Gaining useful knowledge about what policy efforts might work requires a better understanding of the nature of policy processes (Chapter 2), of the nature of sustainability problems (Chapter 3), and some detail of how policy processes can better accommodate this particular set of problems (Chapters 4–10).

Towards an "environmental civics"

A feature of modern sustainability policy rhetoric and debates, and of the late modern era of politics in contemporary societies, is the widening of the "policy community", consistent with advocacy of more inclusive styles of policy-making and politics (Chapter 9). In resource and environmental management, there have been strong moves towards community-based management arrangements, often at local, regional or catchment scales. These moves are welcome, and if well-designed and supported they can be effective. Governments have been very keen on such local, on-ground activity, but they have been less keen on participation in higher level policy processes.

Over recent decades, there have also been strong moves in the field of environmental education, aimed at increasing the community's understanding of environmental issues and thus their capacity to engage in environmentally positive actions. More recently there has been a similar emphasis on education for sustainable development. In both areas, the underlying assumption is that better society-wide outcomes will emerge from a population which understands better the environmental problems we confront and which is aware of specific actions they can undertake. Public education campaigns – termed "moral suasion" by economists – have been a standard policy instrument used by governments over recent decades. Convincing the populace to save water or not litter is obvious, and does not require that political, policy and production systems themselves change.

Through community-based programs and environmental education, as well as through topicality and media coverage of environmental issues, there are many more people aware of the problems than ever before. Yet it is widely perceived that governments, and powerful interest groups, are doing less than they could or should. A subsidiary reason for this book is that I believe a critically important aspect of "education" has been largely overlooked; that is, increasing understanding of how policy is made and implemented, who makes it, and how it could be better made and implemented. Admittedly, policy is a less alluring topic than learning about natural environments or even about environmentally responsible behaviours. However, if environment and sustainability are to be the subject of more inclusive policy process, then sufficient people who understand the policy system and how to engage in it, or how to hold policy-makers accountable, are required.

The general area of public education and understanding to do with policy and politics is known as civics, and it is apparent that in a policy domain characterised by uncertainty and complexity, a "civics education" is doubly important. Hence, part of the aim of this book is to contribute to an *environmental civics*, in the belief that advances in environmental and sustainability policy are more likely to be initiated by non-government individuals and groups rather than governments. That is less a criticism of governments than a simple acknowledgement of the realities of politics in contemporary societies.

Policy and institutions:
Terms and definitions

This book is about two terms – "policy" and "institutions" – and related concepts that are used in different ways by theorists, practitioners and the broader public. For example, in strict theoretical terms an "institution" is an underlying rule or pattern of behaviour in a society, whereas in common use it might mean a specific organisation or even a physical object such as the local bank. Various schools of thought in public policy have quite strict definitions of what a "policy" is, while others have very general understandings. It will become apparent in later chapters that neither term can be tightly and precisely defined, but I will define the meaning they have in this book and try and be consistent in usage from here on:

- *Institutions* are persistent, predictable arrangements, laws, processes or customs serving to structure political, social, cultural or economic transactions and relationships in a society. They may be informal or formal, and allow organised, collective efforts around common concerns. Although persistent, institutions constantly evolve.

- The term *institutional system* conveys the fact that it can be limiting to concentrate on single institutions. Institutions are embedded in complex, interactive systems of many institutions, organisations and actors, and in understanding social and policy change this interdependency must be taken into account.

- *Organisations* are manifestations of institutions, such as specific departments, associations, agencies, and so on. In some cases, an organisation may be persistent, recognisable and influential enough to be regarded as an institution, but generally organisations can be more quickly dissolved or radically changed whereas an institution is more durable.

- *Policies* are positions taken and communicated by governments – "avowals of intent" that recognise a problem and in general terms state what will be done about it. Policies are produced through multi-component and variable *policy processes* that combine government and non-government players. The framework presented in Chapter 4 and detailed in following chapters is a representation of policy processes. The term *policy cycle* is synonymous here with policy process, but emphasises the cyclic and reiterative nature of policy-making.

- *Policy programs* are specific and substantial manifestations of a policy, comprising elements of implementation as well as of intent. Beneath this level, for an applied policy, there will be a variable number of on-ground projects in particular places. For example, a *policy* on river conservation might include, among other things, a *program* of community-based water quality monitoring and remedial works, through which are funded numerous discrete *projects*.

- Public policies are influenced and formulated by multiple *policy actors*, both as individuals and in organised groups. Around any particular issue there will be a discernible *policy community*, comprising all those who have some degree of active involvement and input into policy discussion. Within this, a tighter *policy network* will have responsibility for or power over policy formulation and implementation.

- The concept of *policy sub-systems* is sometimes used to refer to the fact that, within the broader landscape of public policy in a jurisdiction, somewhat separate sets of structures and processes – sub-systems – exist for specific sectors or issues. That is, one can delineate the policy sub-system concerned with environmental policy as opposed to public health policy, or pollution policy and nature conservation policy.

- Within a policy network or sub-system, there are those who are often referred to as "policy-makers" or "decision-makers" – terms that are often used imprecisely. In this book, policy-makers or decision-makers are those who are the *responsible authority*: that is, they have the legal competence and responsibility within the relevant jurisdiction (nation, State or province, local government area, and so on) to make formal policy decisions. The responsible authority may be an individual (for example, Minister or Secretary, senior official with *delegated authority* from government, or a court), or an organisation such as a government department or an industry association or firm.

(However, policies are influenced by many decisions by different actors – see Chapter 2).

- *Policy instruments* are the "tools" used by governments in partnership with other players to implement policies and achieve policy goals; for example a regulation, education campaign or tax (see Chapter 7).

- *Management* is used here to refer to actions taken "on-the-ground", both in implementing a policy instrument and the more tangible physical actions required – policy sets the direction and says how to proceed; management does things to achieve that direction. Managers and policy-makers may be the same individual and more often the same organisation, but the two can also be separate – for example, a government might state a policy on what should happen in conservation reserves, and the statutory parks service or private contractors implement this. *Management regimes* refer to multiple, related components through which management actions take place, including regulations, agencies and official, monitoring programs, funding, and so on.

An example of how such terms might be used in a real situation may help, even though the following is unavoidably generalised and complicated as a result of using almost all the above terms in one brief illustration:

> A land management agency (independent statutory authority, an *organisation* manifesting the *institutions* of the Westminster system of government) has problems with major outbreaks of a noxious weed on the borders of a public forest estate. The agency Director (the *responsible authority*) makes a regulation under the relevant Act allowing weed control spraying to be undertaken at the behest of regional forest managers (*delegated authority*). Neighbouring landholders take legal action objecting to this. Applying the doctrine of nuisance and according primacy to private property rights (*institutions* of the common law) the Supreme Court (*organisation* manifesting core legal institutions) declares the regulation (the *policy instrument*) and thus the weed control (*management actions*) invalid. This prompts considerable discussion in the wider *policy community*, and causes the government to convene a broadly representative advisory body reflecting the relevant *policy network* comprising key government agencies, farmer and

conservation associations and selected scientists, to make recommendations to resolve the issue. The government (political *institution*), acting on this advice and the outcomes of an interdepartmental committee report, Minister's office review and a recent Senate committee report (parts of the *policy process*), announces a new *policy* of inclusive locally-based weed management plans and grants to landholders (new *policy instruments*) that are to be overseen by the Department of Conservation (*management organisation*) and implemented jointly by Department staff and landholders.

Such an example is merely illustrative, and the use and precise meaning of terms will change across situations and jurisdictions. The terminology in the above example – and indeed much of the discussion in this book – is largely consistent with a Westminster system of government such as exists in the United Kingdom, Canada or Australia, as opposed to, say, the system in the United States of America or those more common in continental Europe. As with most descriptions of policy processes and institutional systems, each context is different. However, the approaches presented in this book are adaptable to any political system as long as attention is paid to the local context.

Organisation of the book, and sources

The rest of this book is structured to pursue the aims set out above. The next chapter offers a sharp summary of the discipline of public policy and the practice of policy analysis, without much emphasis on environment or sustainability. Chapter 3 discusses the nature of environment and sustainability issues as policy and institutional problems, and explores why societies are having difficulty addressing them. After consideration of two other policy models, Chapter 4 presents a framework for description, analysis and prescription of policy in the environmental and sustainability domain. This framework is not a "model" of how policy is made or even how it should be made, but rather a checklist and aid for better understanding and making policy. The framework has four main phases – problem-framing, policy-framing, policy implementation and policy monitoring and evaluation – and each contain several more specific elements, along with general elements such as participation and transparency (see Figure 4.2 and Table 4.3).

Chapters 5–9 deal with the four phases and specific elements and with the general elements, describing each and identifying ways in which they can be understood and undertaken. Chapter 10 deals with three particularly difficult aspects of sustainability policy: policy coordination; integrating environmental, social and economic concerns; and institutional change.

Illustrative examples will be used to demonstrate arguments made and the approaches presented. Detailed, more realistic case studies are not used for two reasons. The first is to keep the book as short as possible: useful policy case studies require considerable detail. The second reason is that, whatever the case studies chosen, only a few readers would find the precise detail and context easily transferable to the policy situations they face.

While references are given to provide adequate references for a reader to pursue specific topics further if they wish and to acknowledge where specific ideas have been adopted, the number of references has been limited to keep the length of the volume down. This book is a summarised treatment of a complex and rapidly evolving area, and moreover is one person's version of the topic. Interested readers can, and should, read more widely in the general policy literature and in environmental policy. Overviews of the historical evolution of thinking about environment and sustainability are salutary for their ability to place modern concerns in perspective, including Boyden (1987) and McNeill (2001). The next chapter's short coverage of public policy can be extended by a standard policy text such as those by Howlett and Ramesh (2003) or Colebatch (1998), or by reference to international journals such as *Policy Sciences*, *Policy Studies*, or the *Journal of Public Policy*. Sources more specific to a given country should also be consulted; for example, in Australia, Bridgman and Davis' (2001) concise handbook is invaluable (and was one inspiration for the structure of this book), and the *Australian Journal of Political Science* and *Australian Journal of Public Administration* contain more detailed and specific studies. Each of the specific elements covered in Chapters 5–9 are also the subject of extensive literatures, and the challenges of policy integration and institutional change for sustainability are discussed in a recent but rapidly growing literature. Key references are given in these areas.

On environmental and sustainability policy, this book offers a different approach and coverage than most others, but as befits a complex, topical policy domain there is a rapidly expanding literature. Some general policy journals deal with environmental topics, but sources such as the *Journal of Environmental Management*, *Environmental Science and Policy*, the *Journal of Environmental Assessment, Planning and Management, Global Environmental Change*, or *Ecological Economics* concentrate on environment and sustainability. Books such as Paehlke and Torgerson (1990), Carley and Christie (2000) and Pellikaan and Van Der Veen (2002) are relevant. In terms of general books at the international level that deal with environment and sustainability, the collections edited by Berkhout et al (2002), Page and Proops (2003) and Lafferty (2004) are recent and excellent surveys. Again using Australia as an example, more detailed country-specific discussions of environmental policy are available, such as Dovers and Wild River (2003) or Stewart and Jones (2003), or the *Australasian Journal of Environmental Management*, the *Australasian Journal of Natural Resources Law and Policy*, or the *Environmental and Planning Law Journal*.

Beyond such formally published and accessible sources, the policy field is full of "grey literature", such as conference proceedings or government reports that are invaluable sources of detail and cases. Also, many governments or agencies have policy handbooks or manuals, or written procedures for particular tasks such as policy evaluation. So, while this book can serve as an introduction and guide, there is no shortage of material for those wishing to either delve more deeply or consider different approaches than the one taken here.

Chapter 2

THINKING ABOUT POLICY

This chapter offers an abridged summary of how public policy has been approached over recent decades, of how different perspectives understand the nature of policy, and ongoing issues in public policy of relevance to environment and sustainability. While it is apparent that traditional policy-oriented disciplines and professions have difficulty gaining purchase on sustainability problems it would be foolish to overlook the understanding that has developed over many years in public policy, public administration, law, economics, political science and other areas. A tendency to ignore basic policy knowledge from other areas is a weakness of much environment and sustainability policy thinking. This chapter discusses the links between different disciplines and political ideologies, and their ways of understanding the world in terms of practical policy options and instruments. The discussion then moves on to why policy processes and the knowledge systems that underpin them might fail to achieve what they attempt.

This book is concerned with *public* policy; that is, processes and decisions enabled, made and/or coordinated by government and other institutions operating in the public domain.[1] While the role of other parts of the policy community – firms, stakeholder groups and the wider community – is a core consideration, there is less emphasis on the private sector.

Public policy analysis: Why, who and how?

Although the following discussion is focused on recent times, thought and action on what we now term "public policy" has deep

---

1   This is for two reasons, neither of which should be taken to discount the importance of the private sector. First, sustainability is essentially a long-term social goal, where even in market-oriented economies the primary vehicles for change are collective, public or community institutions. So, while many policy options and processes considered in later chapters involve the private sector, the second reason is that proper consideration of the role of industry sectors and private firms is a quite different undertaking and would enlarge the book beyond the intended length and detail.

historical roots. Well before the rise of what became the modern nation state in the 19th century, governments existed in many forms, and made decisions and implemented actions for common purposes (Finer 1997). The philosophy of democratic government emerging from Ancient Greece onwards is one starting point, but many traditional societies before that had collective institutional arrangements and decision-making processes. Indeed, in recent years in the environment and sustainability domain, the relevance of traditional approaches to government have become a matter of considerable interest, especially in the area of common pool resource management (for example, Dolšak et al 2003). Formal academic disciplines focusing on policy have existed for centuries, with ideas and debates in classical economics, philosophy and politics still relevant.

Modern policy research gained shape in the second half of the 20th century, as social scientists attempted to contribute to the better achievement of emerging social goals by applying more rigour and expertise ("craft") to the "art" of politics and government (for example, Lasswell 1951). They undertook this quest in response to the increasing complexity of both modern societies and economies, and of the range and scale of policy activities that governments were undertaking in the era of post-war reconstruction and of interventionist, Keynesian economic thought.

The field of practice and of academic study is variously called policy analysis, policy sciences, political science, public administration and, most often, *public policy*, with different intentions and directions evident. Over the years thinking about policy has expanded, with a myriad of sub-sets and competing approaches.[2] To explore the field for the purpose here, we can consider four matters: who does policy analysis and what sort of ideas influence the way they do this; what the intent of it is; what they do; and what "enduring questions" persist in theory and practice. Thus we will cover both the more theoretical end of the multi-disciplinary field of public policy, where underlying ideas and assumptions can be discerned, as well as the more practical end where models of policy-making will be encountered.

First, who thinks about policy? Brunner (1991) gives one version, identifying "distinguishable parts of the [policy] movement":

---

2   The full range of the approaches cannot be covered here; see, for example, Daneke (1989); Brooks and Gagnon (1990); Howlett and Ramesh (2003); Fischer (2003).

- public affairs (philosophy);
- policy analysis (economics);
- management science (public and business administration);
- policy studies (political science);
- socio-economics (sociology).

This casts the net broadly in terms of disciplines, but there are others including lawyers and institutional theorists. Government officials and non-government actors may have no particular disciplinary affiliation but certainly "do" policy research as well as make or advocate policy. "Public policy" is a recognisable area of research, training and professional practice. Yet it is an interdisciplinary field rather than a discipline in its own right, as it draws on a number of disciplines, especially political science, economics, law and public administration. In the environment and sustainability domain there are other sub-disciplines and alliances that analyse or prescribe policy to some extent; environmental politics, ecological economics, resource management, and so on. Natural scientists such as ecologists and atmospheric chemists are increasingly liable to examine policy problems and prescribe solutions. The key point is that there are many disciplines and groups involved in policy research. These organise and communicate in various ways, and have varying approaches to defining and analysing policy problems and prescribing solutions. Beneath these differences lie divergences in theories and assumptions about significant things such as how governments work and how human beings are motivated.

The intent of policy analysis varies depending on the aim, the methods, and the affiliation of those involved. A simple split is between that which is *descriptive*, and that which is *analytical*, and across these the extents to which *prescription* is attempted. Hogwood and Gunn (1984: 29) identified two categories – policy studies (a more neutral pursuit) and policy analysis (a more purposeful pursuit) – that overlap in the area of evaluation:

Policy studies
- study of policy content;
- study of policy process;
- study of policy outputs;
- evaluation.

Policy analysis

- evaluation;
- information for policy-making;
- process advocacy;
- policy advocacy, with either –
  - analyst as political actor
  - political actor as analyst.

This raises two relevant distinctions. The first is the difference between analysis that recommends actual policy options or instruments, and that recommending *processes*. Second, and related, is the position of the analyst or researcher, and whether they will be playing what may be seen as a "political" role, driven by normative or value-based concerns. Further, the distinctions made in the typology above allow identification of the intent of proposed analysis: to yield information about policy instruments, to examine implementation and outcomes, or to examine process?

The general approaches employed in thinking about policy are many and varied. A categorisation is presented in Table 2.1 that is concerned with the theoretical basis rather than the more obvious methods and prescriptions. This assists in understanding the underlying differences and linkages between disciplines, political ideologies and policy preferences.

Table 2.1: Approaches to policy and politics

Unit of analysis	Method of theory construction	
	Deductive	Inductive
Individual	Rational choice theories (public choice)	Sociological individualism (welfare economics)
Collective or group	Class analysis (Marxism)	Group theories (pluralism/corporatism)
Structure (institutions)	Actor-centred institutionalism (transaction cost analysis)	Neo-institutionalism (statism)

Source: Howlett and Ramesh (2003: 22)

More deductive approaches tend to apply generalised theories and thus solutions across a range of specific cases they encounter, whereas inductive approaches draw insights from observation of specific cases and may be more wary of applying these across different contexts. Consider some examples from Table 2.1. Public choice approaches are largely utilised by economists, a discipline which attaches great emphasis on the "invisible hand" theory where individual expression of choices through markets is a fundamental force and prime policy lever (see, for example, Gillroy and Wade 1992; Common 2003). This approach has a strong tendency to recommend market mechanisms in a general sense. Approaches more in the pluralism/corporatism category examine the interactions of groups in real situations, although not blind to the role of individuals, and while recommending some policy solutions, these are more about the improvement of processes for such political interactions and have a strong sensitivity to different contexts. Political scientists would be more likely to be found in this cell, and might utilise an approach along the lines of the influential "advocacy coalition framework" designed to allow more structured investigation of the role of policy actors in shifting coalitions (Jenkins-Smith and Sabatier 1994). Such approaches deepen understand of how policy processes work in a social and political sense, but tend not to offer guidance in terms of policy formulation and prescription.

With its emphasis on *public* policy processes and institutional systems, this book comes more out of the "statist" school of thought compared to, say, approaches to institutional systems that focus more on individual and economic transactions (for example, North 1990). However, as with all such categories, there is often overlap, and a particular author, approach or indeed actual policy process will usually evidence the influence of more than one school of thought.

Ongoing arguments over which of these approaches is the best are not of interest here. The styles of approaches to politics and policy in Table 2.1, and others besides, all have some validity, will be observed in policy systems, and are worthy of being better understood and incorporated into policy analysis. To continue the discussion, we can note some further, less theoretical, approaches to policy, not to map the full terrain but simply to indicate how different perspectives might be brought to bear on more "applied" approaches to environment and sustainability policy. Moving towards the more practical end of public policy with which Part II of this book will deal, there are other distinct areas of activity:

- *Policy/program evaluation.* This is the practical side of policy research; where discrete policies or policy programs are assessed for their efficacy, outputs, costs, and so on. This may be carried out within government (in-agencies or by an audit or similar office) or by consultants or non-government actors. This topic is further discussed in Chapter 8.

- *Legal policy research.* Legal research to some degree always entails policy and institutional research. An important distinction is between "legalistic" approaches to regulation, liability, administrative law, and so on, and more "institutional" approaches looking at the law's role in establishing and maintaining institutions and processes and the codification of principles. These issues will be addressed in Chapters 7 and 10.

- *Policy cycle and decision process approaches.* This set of approaches, covered in Chapters 4–9 stem from early work by Lasswell (1951), who proposed a "policy sciences" approach. Initially, the focus was on applied linear "problem-solving" stages of the policy process, to add rigour and purpose to policy analysis and formulation, whereas in more recent times an iterative "policy cycle" approach has become dominant. Typical versions of the linear and cycle approach are matched by Howlett and Ramesh (2003: 11):

Problem-solving phases	*Policy cycle stages*
problem recognition	agenda-setting
proposal of solution	decision-making
choice of solution	policy formulation
putting solution into effect	policy implementation
monitoring results	policy evaluation

This allows a structured approach to interrogating policy and recognises that policy processes have many parts, problems are less often solved than they are addressed, revisited and re-addressed, and this process can be studied by breaking it into parts to allow detailed focus while at the same time appreciating the broader system. The problem with such "models" of how policy is made is that very rarely is policy made in such a neat way, but rather can be *ad hoc* and messy, with little linear logic. Further, there is the difficulty that policy is rarely contained within one agency or clear process, but more often across many. Decision process appraisal, evolving from the work of Lasswell (1971), pursues more tightly defined "decisions" through various stages (for example, Brunner 1996).

The framework presented in Chapter 4 and applied in Chapters 5–10 emerges from the tradition of public policy that utilises policy process and policy cycle models. Before then, the rest of this chapter will identify and discuss some of the ongoing issues in this sort of approach to public policy. Chapter 3 then considers the particular challenges that arise in the environmental and sustainability domain, and that must be accounted for.

Enduring questions in policy analysis

Public policy is not a stable field, but one where ideas and methods are constantly debated and changing. The following identifies some "enduring questions" that feature in policy research and in policy processes. These have yet to be fully resolved, and are relevant to the construction and implementation of any framework or model of policy processes.[3]

"Policy analysis as handmaiden?" (Horowitz and Katz 1975)

This concerns the relationship between policy analysis and research, which may be undertaken by supposedly independent actors, and the state or its policy agencies. That is, the link between policy analysis and policy formulation (see the typology of Hogwood and Gunn (1984) above, and Garson (1986); Torgerson (1986)). Too close an association with government constrains the breadth and perhaps innovative potential of inquiry, but maximises the likelihood of uptake of results, and *vice versa*. In an applied field such as environment and sustainability, where topical and real issues are always present, policy research and even policy analysis by bureaucrats may be constrained by "capture" within

---

3   The following listing is not exhaustive. Also, some people would state that some of the following should be considered already resolved (in favour of their view or theory).

the narrow range of options defined by a government's ideology and current list of priorities. This equals a balance between relevance and independence.

Policy: rational or non-rational?

There has been a longstanding tension between what can be categorised as "rational-comprehensive" and "incremental" approaches to policy (alternatively, synoptic and anti-synoptic traditions). The former constructs policy as a stepwise and well-defined process attended to in a "scientific" manner producing a "rational" outcome. Incrementalism says this is unrealistic – policy-making and thus analysis is more complex and politically contingent than this – and proposes that we proceed in small, less rational steps.[4] An attractive position is halfway – to recognise the variable process and political nature of policy but not abandon the hope of some rigour and direction – a purposeful incrementalism. Incrementalism may be an accurate description of reality, but not necessarily of how things could happen, and rational models can be very useful as analytical tools (Dye 1983). That is the style adopted in Chapter 4. Other important explanations of how policy is made have been proposed. In one, Etzioni (1967) proposed a "mixed scanning" where an initial broad search for ways forward is followed by a second stage of more rigorous analysis and policy design. In a more negative vein, the "garbage can" model of March and Olsen (1979) portrays policy and decision-making as mixing ends and means in an uncoordinated fashion and in response to short-term imperatives. As with most models, anyone involved in public policy could recognise some reality in these explanations, even if the latter model would not be perceived as a desirable state of affairs.

Few policy texts now follow a rational-comprehensive style, although it is definitely the case that many scientists, activists and members of the public believe that such a defined, linear process does or should occur. It should be noted that many resource and environmental managers and policy-makers are being required to show evidence of adherence to quite detailed and strict procedural frameworks reeking of a rational approach, such as impact assessment processes, risk assessment models, or environmental management systems.

---

4 Lindblom (1959) penned the classic description – "the science of muddling through" – and in 1979 put it that we were "still muddling, not yet through".

Related to the above is the question of the *utility of models*. The literature abounds with descriptive, analytical and prescriptive "models" of the policy process, and choosing between these is problematic as each will determine the questions asked, methods used and information sought. Also, the applicability of many policy models to a specific field such as environment and sustainability may be questionable, given their evolution with reference to other, possibly different policy problems (service delivery, social policy, and so on). Any model – whether quantitative or conceptual, simple or complex – has a theoretical, conceptual or philosophical basis, and clarity as to what particular construction of the policy process analysts and researchers subscribe to or are proposing should be encouraged. For example, a focus on individual choice may ignore institutions and non-economic behaviour, whereas an institutional focus may do the reverse. There is also the risk of taking a model too seriously; as a singular representation of either the way things are or should be. An advisable approach is to utilise a reasonably broad and flexible approach, adapt it to the sector or domain at hand, and clearly state any assumptions or limitations (this is the approach taken here, and is discussed in Chapters 3 and 4).

Politics, values and the state

A core problem with policy analysis is the relationship between policy on the one hand, and politics, political values and the state. Rational studies which ignore politics are as unhelpful as a purely political analysis that focuses on the conflict of the moment and descends into a vicarious spectator sport. Indeed, much environmental "policy" literature is in fact the study of politics, of limited prescriptive or operationally proactive content. Many scientists and stakeholders deride "politics", viewing it as a venal expediency obstructing rational decision-making but, as Davis et al (1993: 257) warn, this is unrealistic:

> Politics is *the* essential ingredient for producing workable policies, which are more publicly accountable and politically justifiable ... While some are uncomfortable with the notion that politics can enhance rational decision-making, preferring to see politics as expediency, it is integral to the process of securing defensible outcomes. We are unable to combine values, interests and resources in ways which are not political.

For those analysing and prescribing detailed policies, the challenge is to impose some order on analysis and prescription and proposed process, while factoring in the political context. In a classic study in resource management, Lee (1993) described the politics of river basin management as "bounded conflict" – recognising the political nature of multiple values but also the need to make inevitable conflict constructive. For policy analysis and formulating the answer is to demand sensitivity to political contexts and pursue analysis capable of improving the penetration of policy debates with a wide variety of legitimate information sources and values, a matter of process and institutional design and communication. This enduring question includes the problematic area of political and community will and the common failure of poor or absent implementation after rhetorical or in-principle policy statements. A focus on policy stressing the preconditions to policy and implementation tasks can help in this regard (see the framework in Chapter 4).

Problem definition

Defining policy problems well avoids applying "pseudo-solutions" to "pseudo-problems" (Dery 1984). It has been stated that the policy literature lacks useful typologies of policy problems that extend beyond nominal categories and simple classifications (Linder and Peters 1989). Too often, we confuse substantive issues (for example, salinity, remnant vegetation protection, urban traffic congestion) with the policy problems these present (in these three cases, for example, how to encourage water efficient irrigation, designing tree clearing regulations, promoting use of public transit). Rather than seeking to classify problem types, we can explore more generic problem features via the *attributes* of policy problems in sustainability, with a view to clarifying the features of problems rendering them different or difficult, and then consider what that means for policy responses (Chapters 3 and 5).

Authority and decision-making

As noted in Chapter 1, in any policy process there will be one or more responsible authorities with the legal or other recognised right and responsibility to make decisions. However, despite the importance of recognising such authority, the fact is that a single "policy decision", and even more so a multi-part policy program, will involve many decisions by different actors. For example, a Cabinet decision to regulate a polluting activity and to mount an associated education campaign will be influenced by separate decisions prior to that point, by senior government officials and by industry and environmental groups who were consulted and by the decision of editors to focus media coverage on the issue. In implementing the policy, many more lesser decisions will be significant, by the responsible Minister or Secretary, government officials, industry partners, consultants engaged in communication, and others. At the "sharp end" of policy implementation, individual decisions to evade regulations or to pay attention to received educational material are central to the success of the policy intervention. Across different situations the identity of these actors will vary enormously, and this makes a general characterisation of what a policy process should look like and who should be involved, difficult.

Policy instrument choice

Too often, instrument choice is a matter of convenience, expediency or disciplinary or ideological bias. Singular instruments are often advocated, when typically a mixture will be needed. Further, rarely do we observe a full menu of instruments assessed via consistent criteria. Across the policy literature, there is little consensus on how to choose the best instrument/mix of instruments, or even over what the menu is (for example, Linder and Peters 1989; Howlett 1991). Partly this is due to the difficulties of being prescriptive across so many areas of application. A challenge is to evolve the art and craft of instrument choice and analysis in a manner specific to sustainability problems (which, it was claimed above, are different and difficult). This is pursued in Chapter 7.

Policy learning
(including policy monitoring and evaluation)

Learning from policy experience and accruing lessons in a positive and proactive way would be expected to be normal practice, but although widely advocated is not well understood or often achieved. Lee (1993: 185) stated that "deliberate learning is possible, though surely uncommon, in public policy". Policy (and institutional and management) learning is central to an adaptive approach to environment and sustainability policy, given pervasive uncertainty and a lack of widely agreed policy options. Learning needs to involve improved understanding and not simply mimicry, according to May (1992), who provides a typology: instrumental policy learning, involving the viability of specific instruments or program design; social policy learning, entailing lessons about the social construction of policy problems, the scope of policy or about policy goals; and political learning, where advocates become more knowledgeable about policy processes and how to advance their arguments. Bennett and Howlett (1992) emphasise *who learns*: government instrumentalities; policy actors; or broader policy communities? For learning to take place, there is the issue of whether appropriate processes and institutions exist. The issue of policy learning is revisited in later chapters.

Role and use of information in policy

The role and use of information in policy is an ongoing matter of discussion in public policy (for example, Lindblom and Cohen 1979). Policy processes draw on information from many sources within government circles, the community and specialist sources such as research bodies. Knowledge-based communities (or epistemic communities) at times play a crucial role in informing policy. The apparent expectation of scientists and activists in the environmental domain that scientific information will be transformed into clear messages that will instruct decision-makers in an unambiguous, obvious fashion is usually not fulfilled. Political expediency, other priorities, the knowledge claims of other experts, and so on, will also come into play. Information in policy is not a value-free commodity – different groups and interests have fundamentally varied views of the world, assumptions about how things work, and claims and rejections of the validity of knowledge – and different rationalities emerge associated with a range of "discourses" (for example, Dryzek 1997). With sustainability problems, the range of knowledge systems and information sources relevant to policy debate is particularly wide; for example, the natural and social sciences, private firms and industry associations, environmental groups and local communities – and within each of these discourses there will be diversity and contest. Coupled with uncertainty and long-time horizons, the role of information in sustainability policy is important, complex and poorly understood (Chapters 4–10).

These "enduring questions" recur in public policy, and are especially relevant to a complex, emerging policy concern such as sustainability. In different ways, each one will be reconsidered and incorporated into the discussion of the nature of environment and sustainability problems in Chapter 3, and in the framework presented in Chapter 4 and the rest of the book. The final sections of this chapter explore a little further how opportunities for policy change occur, and the structure and function of government and other players.

Before that, however, we need to make something very clear. Public policy is about changing peoples' behaviours. Thus, policy is inevitably an activity that verges on *social engineering*. In this book I will use the somewhat harsh terms "policy interventions" and "policy instruments" quite deliberately to make this clear. Even when policy is formulated and implemented in a democratic and inclusive manner in keeping with widespread social goals – as this book recommends it should – there will be some who will be encouraged or forced to change the way they live against their preferences or wishes. Human behaviour is tied to human values, and values are intensely personal and political things, and sustainability has deeply normative or value-laden dimensions. To imagine otherwise would be unrealistic.

Policy change and policy choice

From the discussions above of both alternative models and enduring questions in public policy, it is clear that policy is not always – or even ever – made in a clear, rational fashion featuring adequate knowledge and informed choice. It is also clear that such a situation is highly unlikely in environment and sustainability, given complexity, uncertainty and conflicting understanding and values. Nevertheless, recognising this reality still allows for policy processes to be purposeful, as well informed as possible, and transparent to and understandable by all concerned. This can be enhanced by explicit use of a framework such as that presented in Chapter 4; and also by an understanding of how opportunities for policy change and improvement might occur, and thus, when and how policy choices can be made.

How opportunities for policy change occur is an issue given much attention in the policy literature, and includes considerations such as who sets agendas, the cost of policy options, institutional constraints, urgency, and the idea of "policy windows" (see the influential work by Kingdon (1984)). Policy windows are periods of opportunity or imperative for policy change, most often following a period of reasonable stability in policy style and direction. Such windows vary greatly in kind and degree – in why and how they open and in how big a change in policy is made possible. We can identify two basic types of policy window, *predictable and unpredictable*, and under these two categories recognise some common examples of the kinds of situations where policy windows may open:

- More *predictable* policy windows result from situations such as: the lead-in period to a government's annual budget statement; following review of a policy program or where problems with an existing policy are emerging and recognised; the publication and consideration of a major review such as a regular state of environment report; the finalisation or ratification of an international agreement that will require domestic implementation; or an election whether that returns the old government or a new administration.

- More *unpredictable* policy windows result from events such as: scientific discoveries; unforeseen environmental changes like drought, wild fires or pollution episodes; sudden realisation of policy failure; an unexpected rise in the influence of a particular interest group; and quick changes to international settings such as may occur after a disease or pest outbreak, or an important environmental policy decision within an influential country that affects trade.

This is a summary and a convenient classification, but it provides a basis for understanding the diverse and uneven nature of opportunities for policy change. Policy agendas and actual policy can change quite quickly, even though many environmentally concerned citizens would not perceive that this is the case. Two issues can illustrate. The timing between the scientific discovery of the thinning of the ozone layer, the creation of an international policy regime to attend to this, and actual reductions in the production of the chemicals that cause the problem, was only a few years. Climate change and greenhouse gas emissions were scarcely on policy agendas in the early to mid-1980s, but by the early 1990s were high priority issues (though advances on these issues have been much less than many believe they could have been).

Some policy windows allow the possibility of big changes in policy, such as the election of a new government or a large scale and sudden environmental change. In other cases, the magnitude of possible change will be quite modest, such as in the case of a regular review of an existing program that has not attracted great criticism. Caught in the immediate moment, both policy-makers and stakeholders may see little evidence of change, despite a lot of rhetoric and volatility, and perhaps even evident policy ad hocery and amnesia. But "apparent [policy] volatility can become, in retrospect, the stately march of consistent underlying change" (Davis 1993: 15). Whether the change is sufficient relative to the problems being addressed is another matter, about which opinions differ greatly concerning environment and sustainability.

Different kinds of policy window suit different kinds of policy-making, reflecting the possible applicability of one of the range of models of the policy process discussed earlier. For example, a sharp and sudden opening of a window – say, an unexpected ecological catastrophe combined with highly visible policy failure and great urgency – might well leave no near-term option other than reaching into the "garbage can". A more modest but well-considered incrementalism might be appropriate utilising the window offered by the approach of review and evaluation of a policy program that has some problems but overall a reasonable level of success.

Although informed and well-structured policy choice is inherently difficult in the face of unpredictable policy windows where there may be a need for quick answers, there are three ways in which we may be better prepared. The first is to recognise that uncertainty, complexity and long time horizons mean that environmental policies are *experiments*, that they therefore must evolve and change, and that this reality should be built into policy processes and institutional settings (Chapter 3). The second flows from that: understanding that the informing stages *before* developing and implementing a policy, and the monitoring and learning stages *after* implementation, are very important. The third is to recognise that policy windows do open, at times unexpectedly, and thus it is important to have proposals for alternative policies available and discussed regularly, to avoid the rushed and poor choices inherent in the "garbage can" model. For this to happen, policy processes need to be open and for there to be good connections between policy monitoring, environmental monitoring, policy research, and discussion in the wider community.

No matter how well-prepared we might be for moments of opportunity for policy change, it has to be emphasised that policy can never be so rational as to delete the political and value-based contests and choices that some view as "irrational". Poor knowledge, moral biases, conflicting interests, hidden agendas and the allure of convenient quick answers will always exist. Beyond that, *all policy is political*, and so it should be. This applies particularly to sustainability – although we can address the integration of social, ecological and economic values to some degree (Chapter 10), there will never be a metric which can combine all considerations into a single measure against which all trade-offs and decisions can be judged. Qualitative judgment, whether political in the first instance or eventually legal in assessing the fairness and validity of a decision in a court of law, is the way in which all systems of government and other social institutions make important decisions. It is important to recognise who makes decisions in a particular context, which is explored in the next section.

Public policy:
Responsibility and governments

Moving toward sustainability involves addressing complex tensions and incompatibilities between the three component social goals of ecological integrity, social equity and economic efficiency. These tensions have built up over long periods of time. Policy decisions will be made largely by governments, in political systems that involve the interests, values and knowledge of a variety of actors. No member of a modern society or sector of industry is unaffected by sustainability problems, even if they may evidence little interest in them, and no part of government can believably define sustainability as irrelevant to its area of responsibility. In complex, modern societies and economies, sustainability is a classic collective problem, requiring some form of coordinated approach. To some, the need for collective coordination may suggest a strong role for the state and agencies of government; for others it may suggest a more inclusive and cooperative approach involving public, private and community partnerships. In reality, different approaches will suit different problems, and generally some mixture of the two. But whatever the policy style, it is impossible to reduce the role of government beyond a certain point, as essential elements of government and the state are crucial to providing resources, legitimacy and direction. These include: budget powers; the strong role of publicly-funded research; democratic legitimacy through elections; ability to coordinate across sectors, issues and geographical regions; the legal responsibility of senior government decision-makers; and the power to make laws and to enforce those laws (generally, see Peters and Pierre 2003).

Government thus plays an absolutely central role in environment and sustainability policy, even if highly interdependent with non-government players. Yet the term "government" is inaccurate as shorthand for the state sector and public bodies. Properly, the term refers to the particular administration in power in a jurisdiction at a given time, representative of one or more political parties in a legislature. The broader systems of government and public administration relevant to policy vary widely across jurisdictions, and a summary of all possible variations is impossible. Table 2.2 identifies the key components of government systems that play a role in policy processes. In any specific situation, making sense of policy requires understanding of the relevant landscape of government and public administration at a finer level of detail than shown here.

In environment and sustainability and many other policy sectors, most if not all these components will play some role in a particular policy process, whether through debating social goals, framing policy problems, formulating or informing policies, or implementing and evaluating them. In each category multiple organisations and interests will be involved – several government departments, different non-government organisations (NGOs), a court, research organisations, and so on. The broader public will also play a role, whether as individual voters or through opinions channelled through more organised campaigns or groups (Chapter 9).

That leads to an important distinction, between *government* and *governance*. Understood broadly, government is comprised of those components in Table 2.2, merging into non-government and semi-state institutions. Governance is a term used increasingly to refer to the carriage of public and collective affairs much more

Table 2.2: Key elements of the governing state

Head of state	Same as head of government (eg, President) or separate (eg, monarch or president, with government led by Prime Minister)
Legislature, at national or State/provincial level	Parliament, parliamentary committees, etc
Executive	Leader of government (President, Prime Minister, Chancellor), cabinet, ministers/secretaries, government staff
Public service departments	Eg treasury, environment, transport, defence
Statutory authorities	National parks services, catchment management authorities, environmental protection agencies, research and statistical bureaus, etc (more autonomous than departments)
Judicial and regulatory bodies	High or supreme courts, lesser courts, specific bodies eg monopolies commissions, etc
Enforcement agencies	Policy, customs, environmental protection authorities, etc
Local government	Highly diverse in size, mandate, roles
Inter-government mechanisms	National-State/provincial joint bodies, eg, ministerial councils, inter-jurisdictional river basin bodies, etc
Public trading enterprises	Government-owned or controlled bodies, eg, broadcasting corporations, electricity authorities
"Semi-state institutions", private bodies and NGOs	Churches, universities, political parties, etc

After Davis et al (1993)

inclusive of non-government players. In the environment and sustainability domain, the more inclusive notion of governance is very relevant (see Lafferty 2004). This is due to experience to date where policy responses primarily by government or separately by scattered non-government interests have not been adequate to address sustainability problems. It is also relevant as a widely accepted principle of sustainability (see Chapters 3 and 6), and consistent with notions of participatory democracy. Throughout the many groups that are engaged in governance for sustainability, or should be involved, there is a wide perception that policy failure has too often occurred, that policy learning has not occurred often enough, and that a more collective, long-term approach is needed.

Policy failure and learning:
Being "adaptive"

Even official international and national government policy statements admit that policy efforts thus far have not done enough to address sustainability problems. So, policy failure or disappointment is a real problem. However, complete policy failure is as rare as complete success – very few policy interventions fail to achieve any positive change or do not disappoint expectations in some way or produce some unforeseen and unwanted impact. The art is to recognise the experimental and cyclic nature of policy, and to be able to learn from both success and failure. The reasons for failure are many, including poor problem definition in the first place, insufficient information, not recognising uncertainties and risks, imperfect choice of policy instruments, insufficient resources, or a lack of effort in implementation, communication or enforcement. Simple recognition of failure, or of success, is not enough – learning requires identification of such causes and the translation of this knowledge into action.

Open admission of ignorance and/or failure is not a strong feature of all individual humans, and is especially uncommon in modern political systems. Nor is patience and consideration of the longer term. It is personally and politically more rewarding in many circumstances to convey a sense of mastery and certainty and of near-term purpose. Therefore, the "adaptive" approach (or purposeful incrementalism) promoted in this book, and in much sustainability thinking, will be difficult for some people and organisations to adopt as an overall policy style. The adaptive idea comes from the notion of "adaptive management" (AM) developed by ecologists and managers in the face of uncertainty and complexity in managing ecosystems (for example, Holling 1978; Gunderson et al 1995).

Adaptive management suggests that management interventions be framed deliberately as hypotheses, to be applied, tested, monitored and learned from. Although originally developed in the context of defined management experiments, the adaptive style can be proposed for policy processes and institutional settings more generally. To illustrate what an adaptive approach to environment and sustainability policy and institutions might entail, and how an adaptive approach relates to policy failure and learning, the following five principles can be proposed (see further Chapters 3 and 10):[5]

- *Persistence,* because without sufficient longevity in policy and institutional efforts it is doubtful that learning or even realisation of policy success or failure can be achieved.

- *Purposefulness,* addressing goals and applying principles that are widely recognised and endorsed, so that all participants understand the logic of what is being attempted (see Chapters 3 and 5).

- *Information-richness and sensitivity,* because in the face of uncertainty a premium must be placed on the best possible information both in terms of its acquisition and manipulation within policy networks, but importantly of its wider ownership and use amongst the broader policy and general communities.

- *Inclusiveness,* so that the logic of the policy or institutional measure and its impacts and success/failure are understood and can be influenced by a wide range of participants.

- *Flexibility,* or the ability to alter policy and institutional responses in the face of new knowledge or changed circumstances, and so that persistence and purposefulness do not develop into rigid and unchangeable patterns.

These are very general attributes of adaptive policy processes, institutions and management regimes, but they set some directions for how to think about the broad style and direction of environment and sustainability policy. Also, they may be in conflict, and require the balancing and trading off in the manner emphasised earlier as inevitable in a policy area that is political and value-laden. Many people might see them as rather obvious, just as they might see some elements of a good policy process as identified later in this book as obvious. Obvious or not, both the general attribute of informed adaptiveness or the practical matter of good policy process are often enough missing, and policy failure too often observed, for it to be worth thinking carefully why this is this case and how it can be remedied.

---

5   These principles or attributes were developed from a variety of sources, both theoretical and empirical, and utilised in a major review of Australian resource and environmental policy over the past three decades (see Dovers and Wild River 2003).

To introduce the rest of the book, we can propose two essential reasons for policy failure: (a) poor understanding of the problems being addressed; and (b) poor construction of the processes through which policy responses are undertaken. We can restate these as two basic requirements for minimising policy failure and for enhancing policy learning and thus improvement. The first is a clearer understanding of the policy and institutional problems faced with environment and sustainability. That is the subject of the next chapter. The second is a fuller understanding of what would comprise a better policy process for environment and sustainability. Such a framework is presented in Chapter 4 and expanded on in subsequent chapters.

Chapter 3

ENVIRONMENT AND SUSTAINABILITY AS POLICY AND INSTITUTIONAL PROBLEM

This chapter deals with environment and sustainability as a suite of "problems" to analyse and resolve, or at least to move forward on, rather than as a collection of "issues" to be worried about and debated. The implications for policy of the emergence of the sustainability idea are revisited, and the main elements of the current sustainability agenda identified. It then identifies the underlying attributes of policy and institutional problems in sustainability, and the generic challenges that are defined by both stated policy objectives and these attributes. Finally, the main forms of policy response to sustainability are noted, and the need identified for a framework to inform policy analysis and prescription that benefits from an understanding of the particular nature of sustainability problems as well as by traditional policy-oriented disciplines and professions that have difficulty coping with sustainability.

The emergence and meaning of sustainability

Although the statement of sustainability as an agenda for modern policy is quite recent (from the 1992 UN Conference on Environment and Development, see UN 1992), concern over the long-run sustainability of human societies goes back much further.[1] The modern idea of sustainability – as opposed to discrete environmental concerns – can be dated from the classic "Spaceship Earth" essay by the economist Kenneth Boulding (1966), and the modern sustainability debate from 1972 and the first international meeting on environment held at Stockholm and the publication of *Limits to Growth* (Meadows et al 1972). The 1980 World Conservation

---

1   For discussions, see Boyden (1987); Ponting (1990); McNeill (2001), and a number of articles in Volume 1(1) of the journal *Ecological Economics*.

Strategy and subsequent national strategies saw further evolution of understanding of both the problems and the policy challenges. These emerging concerns were brought to prominence by the report of the World Commission on Environment and Development (1987) *Our Common Future*, which built upon previous United Nations processes dealing with environment, human development and poverty, and security. Further back, concern over resource depletion is very old, from Ancient Greece through to the 18–19th century classical economists, and including many traditional societies that incorporated concern for natural systems in myth and law.

Returning to the modern policy agenda as stated in international agreements and in much national policy, we can discern some common and central elements (see Chapter 6 for more detail):[2]

- An overall objective of a pattern of economic and human development that does not damage the opportunities for future generations to use natural resources and enjoy a healthy environment, while allowing for human development goals, especially for the world's poor, to be met in the near term.

- Recognition of major social and policy goals, generally including:
    - the importance of biodiversity and ecological life support systems;
    - the need to treat environment and development in an integrated way rather than as separate, competing considerations.

- Guiding principles for policy and decision-making, generally including:
    - factoring in both short and long-term considerations;
    - integrating environmental, social and economic concerns in policy-making;
    - taking precautionary measures in the face of uncertainty and possible serious environmental degradation (the Precautionary Principle);

---

2   The following draws on international documents such as the 1992 Rio Declaration, and the way in which such statements have been translated into domestic policy in various countries.

- considering global implications of domestic policy directions;
- utilising innovative, new policy approaches, such as participatory management, institutional change and market mechanisms; and
- involving communities in decisions that affect them.

These are higher level, vague instructions and many international and national policy statements, and many more statements by interest groups, give more detail and specific targets and actions. In this book, the emphasis is less on what such detail and targets are or should be, than on the sorts of processes that would allow the general goals and principles above to be better pursued. For any individual in a policy agency or interacting with a government, the specific policy agenda of that sector and jurisdiction will be a primary reference point for what can be discussed and achieved. Later in this chapter, these general principles will be translated into policy challenges.

These apply across the suite of substantive issues that were identified in Table 1.1, meaning that a large number of issues and problems may be on a policy agenda, as well as a number of principles and ideas for how to handle those problems. To assist with sorting and understanding this potentially confusing array of issues and principles, Table 3.1 uses a specific example to identify different kinds and levels of considerations that will be encountered in environment and sustainability policy (see further Chapter 5), and an example relevant to another higher-order social goal: public health.

The important distinction made in Table 3.1 is between a *substantive issue* (observed or predicted situation perceived as undesirable) and the restatement of this as one or more *policy problems* (tractable and amenable to a policy response).

Issues *versus* problems: The attributes of sustainability problems

The "issues" that comprise sustainability were detailed in Table 1.1. From a policy perspective such substantive issues are only the beginning of the process of identifying and clarifying policy problems that we can then address through policy processes. Issues are for being concerned about and debating, problems

Table 3.1: Hierarchy of goals, issues, policy problems

	Example 1	Example 2
Social goal	*Public health*	*Sustainability*
Substantive issue (example)	Sub-standard health outcomes in disadvantaged households	Climate change
Policy problem (selected)	Increase access/use of medical services by poor	Reduce energy-related greenhouse gas emissions
Policy principles (selected)	Equity of access; efficiency in public expenditure	Polluter/beneficiary pays; precaution; equity; regional economic considerations
Policy (selected)	Universal health scheme	Prices in energy sector to reflect environmental costs
Policy actions/instruments (selected)	Income-tested health services card entitling holder to reduced cost services; subsidies to doctors; information campaign	Carbon tax at "well-head"; enabling legislation; tax revenue funds adjustment grants to energy-producing regions and rebates for poor households

are for resolving. Two examples can illustrate this (see discussion on element 8, Chapter 5).

"Climate change" or "the enhanced greenhouse effect" are major issues in sustainability, but they are not policy problems. They are biophysical phenomena predicted by science, with an array of natural and human induced causes and impacts on natural and human systems, and with much associated detail and uncertainty. While a policy process may be organised to address these issues, the issues are not tractable or meaningful policy problems themselves. Flowing from predictions of climate change are many *policy problems*, such as reducing per capita use of fossil fuels to thus reduce greenhouse gas emissions, protecting low-lying lands from inundation, or diversifying agricultural production systems in the face of likely regional climate shifts.

Similarly, "biodiversity" is a scientific construct involving various ways of measuring the diversity of non-human life (genetic, species, ecosystem), and the idea that maintaining such diversity is important for the functioning of natural systems and maintenance of services that such systems supply to human societies (see Wilson 1994). It also represents the idea that other life forms and natural ecosystems have innate value. "Protecting biodiversity" is a social goal, associated with which are a large number of actual policy problems, such as regulating illegal wildlife harvests, or providing incentives for farmers to retain native vegetation on their land. (Chapter 5 uses biodiversity as an example of more detailed problem-framing.)

Identification and discussion of issues (usually in the form of valued assets or problematic environmental change) is an important element of the broader policy process (Chapters 4 and 5), and precedes the translation of these concerns into tractable policy problems. Another critical element and linkage in environment and sustainability policy is for reiteration between issues and problems and responses through environmental and policy monitoring, whereby understanding of issues will change over time, as will our construction of policy problems and of the necessary policy responses. At all these levels, an understanding of the nature of these issues and problems is required, of grasping the features that shape the problems and the challenges they represent.

Many people concerned with the policy and research agendas of sustainability feel or claim that the issues it contains are particularly difficult ones, although the reasons why this is the case are less often made clear. So, what are the features of issues and policy problems in sustainability that we need to recognise from a policy perspective, and what are the attributes that determine how we might tackle them? Table 3.2 summarises the key attributes of policy problems in sustainability, noting that not all are evident for any one issue or problem, and that many are interrelated.

The following points explain the attributes. After that explanation, two considerations that arise are discussed: the implications of sustainability problems being different in kind and perhaps degree to traditional problems in public policy, and the cross-problem difficulties and opportunities that are defined by identifying these underlying attributes.

Table 3.2: Attributes of policy problems in sustainability

1. Broadened, deepened and variable spatial and temporal scales.
2. Possible absolute ecological limits to human activities, and threshold effects.
3. Often cumulative rather than discrete environmental impacts of human activities.
4. Irreversible impacts, and related policy urgency and high stakes.
5. Complexity within and connectivity between problems, both within and across the three arenas of environment, society and economy.
6. Pervasive risk and uncertainty, and a lack of or poor quality information.
7. New moral dimensions, specifically non-human species and future human generations, and multiple interests and values.
8. Systemic rather than simple problem causes, embedded in patterns of production, consumption, settlement and governance.
9. Lack of available, uncontested research methods, policy instruments and management approaches.
10. Assets not traded in formal markets and thus not assigned economic value.
11. Poorly defined policy, management and property rights, roles and responsibilities.
12. Mixture of public and private costs and benefits.
13. Strong demands and justification for increased community participation in both policy formulation and environmental management.
14. Sheer novelty as a suite of policy problems.
15. Need for new, integrative/interdisciplinary research.

Source: Dovers (1997)

1. *Spatial and temporal scale.* Natural systems have many processes and functions that operate over extended time horizons and geographical scales. Geomorphic and ecological change in disturbed rivers, the build up of salinity following irrigation or land clearance, accumulation of pollutants or nutrients in soils or aquatic systems, population declines in long-lived species, and so on – these processes may occur over decades before problems become obvious, and by which time remedial policy or management interventions may be difficult. Similarly, natural processes, and human impacts on them, have no respect for political or administrative boundaries, such as is the case with downstream impacts of human activity, harvesting of migratory species, or acid rain across borders from the pollution sources. This presents challenges to human observation, understanding and policy processes that are short term or are contained within a particular jurisdiction.

2. *Possible ecological limits and thresholds.* In some cases, absolute limits may exist as a constraint to human activity – the shortage of space or a resource, the absolute limit of an ecosystem to absorb wastes, and so on. Although a problematic notion that has been contested strongly ever since *Limits to Growth* (Meadows et al 1972), the prospect exists and presents a challenge to policy. Moreover, it is understood that the dynamics of natural systems, and natural systems under human pressure, may exhibit non-linear and non-equilibrium behaviours, meaning that sudden changes may occur rather than steady and predictable change. For example, a fish stock may appear sustainably harvested, but a threshold of reproduction is reached and a sudden decline occurs. Or, the capacity of an aquatic system to assimilate nutrient inputs is reached, with the sudden appearance of algal blooms.

3. *Cumulative impacts.* The examples of thresholds just given illustrate cumulative impacts, but there are many other kinds, such as slow loss of scenic or recreational amenity from development or from increasing visitation, or the slow but steady build up of atmospheric pollution, or heavy metals in the soft tissues of wildlife. This is the "death of a thousand cuts" problem. The attribute of cumulative impacts ties closely to (1) above, temporal scale, and demands long-term policy thinking and assessment of impacts at more than the scale of single development projects.

4. *Irreversible impacts.* In some cases, environmental degradation may be irreversible, whether in absolute terms (for example, species extinction) or in any practical sense or time horizon (for example, serious loss of topsoil where soil formation will take millennia). This sets a limit to experimentation with management regimes if the possible environmental impacts are irreversible and thus cannot be rectified if we get it wrong (see discussion of "serious and irreversible" impacts and the precautionary principle in Chapter 5).

5. *Complexity and connectivity.* Few environmental or sustainability issues can be treated in isolation, as they are connected in cause or effect to other issues. For example, multiple greenhouse gas sources (for example, from land clearance, waste disposal, energy use, and so on) need to be accounted for in any coherent policy. Managing an estuary for recreation

and fisheries production demands linkages to upstream issues such as forestry, agriculture and urban development. Such linkages create complexity that must be understood, and connections between issues that must be accounted for in designing policy and management interventions. As well as connectivity between biophysical phenomenon and use of natural resources, a core logic of the idea of sustainability is connection between environmental, social and economic systems and thus policy.

6. *Risk, uncertainty and poor information.* Although our understanding of natural systems and the implications of human interventions in these systems has improved greatly in recent years, poor information, risks and uncertainties remain highly problematic for policy and management and for public debate. We are uncertain as to the state of the environment, the extent of human impacts on the environment, the long-term implications of those impacts, and the effectiveness of the various policy and management strategies that we are implementing or proposing (see element 6, Chapter 5).

7. *New moral dimensions, multiple values.* Sustainability centres around a concern for the welfare of future generations. Although long-standing ideas such as "posterity" contain a similar concern, sustainability is fundamentally different as it warns not to cut off options for later generations to gain benefits from natural resources and environmental services. This is a relatively recent moral issue, as is the widening of ethical concern for the welfare and innate value of species other than domesticated or charismatic animals and scenic landscapes. These moral concerns have yet to be satisfactorily incorporated into policy considerations (for a discussion, see Attfield 2003). As well, environment and sustainability problems typically evidence different values and expectations of resource access by interested parties, that must be considered in policy-making.

8. *Systemic causes.* The underlying causes of sustainability problems are often located deep in patterns of production and consumption, settlement and governance. Illustrative examples include: fossil fuel use which is fundamental to the operation of modern economies and is tightly linked to greenhouse gas emissions, urban congestion and air pollution;

government structures and divisions of responsibility that do not easily account for environmental considerations; and land tenure and property rights institutions that make common pool resource management difficult. Such deep-rooted causes are often resistant or costly to change (Chapter 5).

9. *Lack of research methods, policy instruments and management approaches.* Researchers, policy-makers and managers alike have an array of approaches available, but little agreement as to the most appropriate and effective, or insufficient evidence or experience upon which choices can be made.

10. *Non-traded and non-valued assets.* In market economies, it is generally things that have economic value that are focused on by policy-makers, firms and individuals. The costs and benefits of use and management of these assets can be assessed, and regular trading of them ensures the generation of information about their quantity and use and provides opportunities for policy interventions. In environment and sustainability, many critical assets are not traded or do not have economic value attached to them, such as air, wildlife species, climate, pollination by insects and birds, and so on. While non-market valuation techniques to assign monetary values to such assets are increasingly available and moves toward creating markets through such means as tradable water rights or fish quota have progressed, many natural assets remain difficult to value (see Chapters 5 and 7).

11. *Ill-defined policy and property rights and responsibilities.* Well-recognised responsibilities for policy and well-defined property rights make it clear to whom responsibilities should be assigned. Many environmental and especially sustainability problems cut across existing policy sectors, jurisdictions, professional and disciplinary domains and land tenures that were defined before these problems became significant. This results in shared responsibilities and often in confusion over who should be responsible.

12. *Public and private costs and benefits.* Resulting from (10) and (11) above, there is usually a mix of public and private costs and benefits involved in environmental management. For example, maintaining or re-establishing native vegetation on private land may benefit the landowner (shade for stock, reduced

erosion and salinity, enjoyment of wildlife), but also has benefits for the general public and future generations (biodiversity, cleaner water in rivers) and for other private landholders (downstream water quality, reduced salinity). Such situations can make it unclear how much of the cost should be borne by private landholders and other direct users, and how much by the government on behalf of society.

13. *Need for community involvement.* For three reasons, greater involvement of the community in environmental and sustainability policy is advocated and expected.[3] First, there is a rising interest in most societies favouring more participatory forms of governance and democracy. Second, local communities and interest groups are demanding and expecting involvement in decisions and actions affecting their environments and the resources they rely on. Third, policy-makers realise that without understanding, support and involvement of the community, policy programs are unlikely to succeed. (And, for some governments, devolving environmental management tasks to local communities may suit their agendas of public sector reductions.) Two interrelated challenges exist: incorporation of civil society into processes of policy formulation, and inclusion or empowerment of local communities in management activities (see Chapter 9).

14. *Novelty.* The policy agenda of sustainability is quite recent, at least in terms of developing a full understanding and of developing well-understood institutional responses. Although many activists would regard sustainability problems as long-standing and be impatient with responses so far, new issues have regularly emerged, understanding has evolved rapidly, and fundamental changes to policy styles and especially institutions generally take a long time. For instance, from the earliest coherent recognition and communication of public health concerns through to their regular incorporation in government programs took, literally, centuries (Boyden 1987). Hopefully competent handling of sustainability problems will not take that long, but societies have yet to get used to how to handle sustainability problems.

---

3   Community, the public, stakeholders, civil society and other terms are often used interchangeably – see further clarification of what constitutes "the community" in Chapter 9.

15. *Integrative/interdisciplinary research.* To comprehend and deal with natural-human system interactions and the merging of environmental, social and economic considerations, there is an increasing demand for collaborative effort across disciplines and other knowledge systems (interdisciplinarity) and for better integration between the domains of science, policy and community (eg, Becker and Jahn 1999).

Some of these attributes are particular to environment and sustainability (for example, ethical concern for other species, ecological thresholds, temporal scale), while others are encountered in other policy domains (for example, uncertainty, public–private costs and benefits, and so on). However, taken together, these problem attributes lead to two important considerations.

First, significant sustainability issues (climate change, biodiversity, population-environment linkages, integrated land and water management, and so on) evidence these attributes more often, and especially more often in combination, than do many other, traditional policy issues (for example, service delivery, economic development). Therefore, *sustainability problems are different in kind* and some might argue in degree to problems in other policy domains. Most of our policy processes, organisations, institutions, professions, skills, and research and analytical approaches have been fashioned against and co-evolved with problems that do not display these attributes so often. Thus there is a prima facie case that existing policy approaches, institutional arrangements and knowledge systems may have difficulty with sustainability problems. This is not to say that other policy problems are "easy", or that existing disciplines are inherently deficient, but that sustainability is a different problem set, and thus will require different knowledge and approaches to policy.

Second, identification of underlying attributes or features of problems encourages us to consider the adequacy of policy responses *across a range of issues and problems,* rather than only considering one at a time. To illustrate, we can consider two cases where separate issues evidence the same problem attributes and thus invite connection in research and policy. Currently, tradable resource rights are being proposed in water management, and have been implemented already to a greater extent in fisheries management. The policy communities and research bodies concerned with these two sectors are largely unconnected, and the argument that rights markets in water might be usefully informed by empirical analysis of the fisheries experience with individual transferable quotas is often met with the comment "that's fish, this is water". However, recognising that common problem attributes (see 10–12 above) are being addressed, rather than keeping the problems isolated in their separate sectors, suggests mutual policy analysis and learning. Similarly, in many natural resource management contexts – including forests, catchments, wastes, and so on – efforts are being made to engage private, government and community interests in partnerships to manage resources, and the industries and values supported by those resources, where attributes 5 and 11–13 are influential. Yet too often, participatory management arrangements are established for one issue, then again and separately for another, and so on.

Thus, the recognition of the common attributes of environment and sustainability problems suggests the need for whole-of-field understanding, capacities and institutional and policy settings. So does the realisation that environment and sustainability represents a new and different policy set of challenges. Some of the core policy and institutional challenges already identified in general terms in existing, official sustainability policy are summarised in the next section.

Policy and institutional challenges

The problem attributes described above allow the restating of the policy and institutional challenges inherent in the modern idea of sustainability and in complex environmental issues in a more detailed fashion. Accepting that major policy change and deeper institutional change will take considerable time, these challenges represent tasks that, if pursued seriously, would allow development of capabilities to deal with sustainability problems.

The aims and principles stated in sustainability policy (see above, and Chapters 1 and 5), are rather general and largely aspirational, and only offer vague direction in terms of policy and institutional reform. Taking these general principles and informing them further via the problem attributes identified above, we can identify more operational policy and institutional challenges. That is, what sorts of changes would render policy processes and institutional settings more suited to progressing the social goal of sustainability? While still generic, the challenges and tasks in Table 3.3 are more detailed and stated in a positive fashion.

**Table 3.3: Environment and sustainability:
Policy and institutional challenges**

Summary	Explanation: policy and institutional settings that ...
1. Long-term policy	Give greater emphasis to longer-term ("supra-electoral") considerations alongside nearer-term imperatives.
2. Inter- and intra-generational equity	Require and/or enable explicit balancing and/or integration of equity considerations across generational time spans.
3. Global dimensions	(a) Recognise and act upon global dimensions of sustainability problems, and (b) Connect domestic and international information strategies, understanding, policy processes and institutions.
4. Policy integration	Allow and/or enforce integration and joint analysis of environmental, social and economic factors and policy.
5. Biodiversity and ecological processes	Place an explicitly higher priority on protection and management of biodiversity and underlying ecological processes.
6. Information focus	Encourage and/or demand high priority on information gathering, dissemination and use, and connections between information systems and policy processes.
7. Precaution	Mandate pro-environment and pro-sustainability decisions in the face of uncertainty (proactive rather than reactive policy).
8. Inter-jurisdictional	Where necessary, allow and/or enforce management, policy and institutional responses across political, geographic and administrative boundaries.
9. Participation	Encourage and enable the participation of interested and affected members of the public in policy and management.
10. Innovative policy approaches	Encourage, enable and experiment with innovative policy approaches, such as information-based strategies, institutional reform, participatory arrangements, community-based management and market-based instruments.

In Chapter 6, more precise policy principles are identified. For now, the challenges in Table 3.3 can serve as a basis for noting the nature of policy and institutional responses to the sustainability agenda thus far.

Responses thus far

Policy and institutional responses around the world vary significantly across both jurisdictions and issues and sectors. Conveying that detail here is impossible but some overall comments are possible (see OECD, various years). At the broadest level, the number of international policies and agreements on environment and sustainability has been impressive over the past decade or two, even if the implementation and strength of these agreements has attracted much criticism (for reviews, see Stokke and Thommessen 2001; Elliott 2004). These agreements range from general ones on sustainability (for example, emerging from Rio in 1992 and Johannesburg in 2002), through global agreements on issues such as fisheries, forests, biodiversity and climate change, to countless more specific regional or bilateral agreements. Less impressive, but still positive and noticeable, has been the implementation of such agreements at the national level.

The majority of national and sub-national (state, provincial) governments have some kind of sustainability (or sustainable development) policy, implemented to a greater or lesser degree (see Lafferty and Meadowcroft 2000; Swanson et al 2004). Sectoral or issue-defined policies exist in great abundance, across greenhouse, biodiversity, fisheries, pollution, energy, and so on. Again, these are more obvious in their existence than in their implementation. In terms of the policy styles and instruments used to give effect to policies, the traditional mainstays of environmental policy – regulation and education driven by government – have mostly increased in their application, although the adequacy of both have come under question. This questioning recognises the complexity of the causes of unsustainable behaviours, and seeks to address the incentive structures and other determinants of such behaviours rather than simply issuing instructions. What are sometimes termed "new environmental policy instruments", including self-regulation by industry and partnership approaches involving multiple interest groups, are increasingly favoured (for example, Gunningham and Grabosky 1999; Sterner 2002). The involvement of communities in on-ground management activities and to a lesser extent by stakeholder groups in policy formulation, have also become more popular policy styles. Finally, the use of market mechanisms (or price or economic instruments) is widely advocated and recently these have been increasingly implemented.

At the institutional and organisational levels, there has been an increase in experimentation with new organisational forms, such as "mega-departments" that combine multiple relevant sectors, integrated catchment management bodies, inclusive national councils for sustainable development (NCSD), and whole-of-government mechanisms including commissioners for environment or offices of sustainability within central agencies (Chapter 10). The design and use of "multi-stakeholder partnerships" has been a strong trend especially in developing countries where such approaches are seen as providing the institutional capacity otherwise in short supply. However, in both the developed and developing worlds, the institutionalisation of such partnerships in terms of mandate, resources and permanence has not progressed far. Overall, sustainability has yet to become a core consideration in public policy, and has lacked the sort of institutional structures that would make it an equal priority along with other (especially economic) policy imperatives.

In judging that responses thus far fall well short of what is required, the evidence for this is three-fold: that many environmental and human development problems continue to worsen; that many informed commentators are of this opinion; and that even official national and international policy statements say this. But how much is needed? A common debate in the sustainability literature revolves around the idea of "weak" versus "strong" sustainability. This refers to a distinction in economic approaches to sustainability defined by *substitutability*.[4] Weak sustainability assumes that natural capital (resources, species, assimilative capacity, and so on) can generally be substituted by human-made capital, thus sustaining human well-being over time. The position of strong sustainability proposes that natural capital cannot always or even mostly be substituted by human-made capital, with the implication that limits to human use of resources and environmental assets are real and close. In reality, proponents of the weak version of sustainability would admit some limits to substitutability (for example, a liveable climate), and those of the strong version would admit that some natural capital may indeed be sacrificed, and so rather than a clear distinction a continuum exists. But it is certainly the case that the vast bulk of policy responses thus far are at the "weak sustainability" end of the spectrum.

---

4   For a discussion of this and other economic approaches to sustainability, specifically written for non-economists, see Common (1995).

We can extend this line of thought to policy and institutional responses to sustainability as similarly being toward the weak or strong ends of a spectrum. Weak responses entail statements of problem recognition and intent, but proceed through existing or slightly amended capacities of standard institutional structures and policy processes, and largely unchallenged knowledge systems represented by professions and disciplines. Stronger responses recognise the unique nature of the problems, and both the inadequacy of policy, institutional and intellectual capacities and the fact that these are causes of unsustainability, and seek to change patterns of production and consumption, settlement and governance. In those terms, policy commitments so far, and even more so institutional responses, have been closer to the weak end. This book does not judge how much more needs to be done other than to note that it is widely believed that significantly more effort is required. Rather, it concentrates on how the policy wherewithal can be created to allow a stronger response to happen, or to decide whether such a stronger response is in fact required.

Beyond rhetoric: Before and after the "policy statement"

To allow a stronger response, or to decide the degree of response needed, it is necessary to look beyond the most common response type – a poorly-implemented policy statement focused on an issue – towards what comes before and after such a policy. Sustainability is a complex problem set, and thinking about sustainability is aided by the detail and rigour made possible by recognising the problem attributes and policy challenges above. Policy is similarly complex, and we need similar detail in thinking about what might comprise an adequate policy process. The next chapter draws on standard policy thinking (Chapter 2) and the nature of sustainability problems (this chapter) to develop a framework for describing, analysing and prescribing environment and sustainability policy.

Chapter 4

POLICY CYCLES AND MODELS, ENVIRONMENT AND SUSTAINABILITY

This chapter first deals with the usefulness of models of policy processes, in particular more recent constructions of policy cycles, and discusses the issues involved with applying such models to sustainability problems. The chapter then presents the policy framework used to structure the rest of the book, combining the strengths of standard policy models with an appreciation of the particular characteristics of the environment and sustainability domain, and makes clear the limitations of the framework. Finally, it emphasises the interdisciplinary nature of sustainability by identifying the different disciplines and other knowledge systems that have relevance to each element of the policy process.

Policy: rational or chaotic?

Revisiting Chapter 2, recall the major ways of characterising policy-making processes that have been influential: the linear, mechanistic rational-comprehensive model; the more humble and less proactive incrementalism; the pragmatic mixed scanning approach; and the pessimistic and chaotic garbage can model. We can also recall the problems and strengths of each "model" of the reality of policy-making, and that all have partial merit for different purposes. In reality, something like the mixed scanning approach, or a purposeful incrementalism is probably the best we can hope for, but informed by a more detailed and "rational" ideal and recognition of the reiterative nature of policy and its political context. Such a position is realistic, and suited to sustainability and the need to be adaptive.

Policy is sometimes simple and linear, sometimes it is a chaotic mess, mostly, it is somewhere in between, and invariably complex. Recognising that, we still need ways to engage with policy and make sense of a variable reality: such a device is usually called a model. But also recall from Chapter 2 that one can take models too seriously. Models are a representation of what we think reality is like. Obviously, with multiple valid models, if we adhere too firmly to one of them, then most of the time we will be wrong. So, rather than a "model" that we might end up thinking is real, or even thinking *can* be real, we might think of diagrammatic or tabular summaries of the policy process as *parables* – useful and informative ways of thinking about the world, but not necessarily likely or true. However, recognising that the term "policy parable" is not a viable term, "framework" will be used here: we need a flexible framework that prompts us to think about what comprises a comprehensive policy process, and which can be used for descriptive, analytical or prescriptive purposes. The next section considers two good, standard frameworks (models), before detailing the one used in this book.

Two policy models

To clarify requirements for a framework for characterising and further exploring environment and sustainability policy, we can consider two different policy cycle models. The five basic stages in a policy cycle identified by Howlett and Ramesh (2003) presented in Chapter 2 are typical of the content of many models and descriptions of the policy cycle. These stages are identified and defined in Table 4.1. Remembering the complexity of policy-making discussed in Chapters 2 and 3, and that the sort of model shown in Table 4.1 is very much a summary of such complexity (and the authors stress this), a more detailed model of the policy cycle is both possible and for many purposes necessary. Figure 4.1 shows a more detailed model, the "Australian policy cycle" from Bridgman and Davis (2001).

Although useful, these two models and many similar ones do not quite suit the purpose of this book. This is not a criticism of the models, especially taken in summary forms and out of their explanatory context as they are here, but to illustrate that we need different ideas and constructions of the policy process to handle sustainability problems. The first model in Table 4.1, as an iteration of the basic parts of a policy cycle, is a good summary, but it begs further detail (the rest of the book it comes from is a fine exposition of that detail). However, neither it nor the second model is specific to environment and sustainability. For example, the stages of "agenda-setting" or "issue identification" do not define the environmental

Table 4.1: Stages in the policy cycle

Stages in the policy cycle
1. *Agenda-setting*, where problems come to the attention of governments.
2. *Policy formulation*, where policy options are developed within government.
3. *Decision-making*, where governments adopt a particular course of action.
4. *Policy implementation*, where governments put policies into effect.
5. *Policy evaluation*, where results are monitored, and problems and solutions reconsidered.

Source: Howlett and Ramesh (2003)

Figure 4.1: The policy cycle

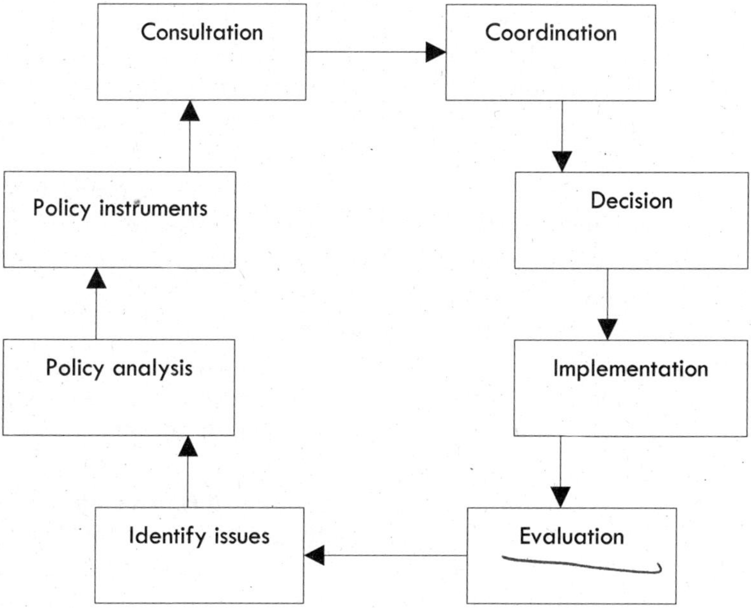

Adapted from Bridgman and Davis (2001)

57

monitoring or social debate over inter-generational equity that must occur in sustainability.

The second model has the further detail that is required to inform policy-making. However, some elements are of questionable applicability to the sustainability context. For example, the stage of "identifying issues" needs further, explicit explanation when uncertainty and poorly defined problems are typical and problem definition is a more complex matter, as is the case with sustainability. Similarly, the placing of "consultation" after the problem identification stage, and after "policy analysis", is not suited to complex policy problems where more participatory approaches need to be explicitly required from the stage of defining problems. It assumes that debate over social goals has occurred sufficient to direct policy-making, yet this is not the case with sustainability.

To consider in more detail the elements of a comprehensive construction of policy processes for environment and sustainability, some preconditions exist:

- First, given that a strict *model* is an inadvisable construction of policy reality, it is better to think in terms of a *framework* for describing, analysing and prescribing policy, made up of *elements* that are often but not always undertaken in a strict or regular sequence.

- Second, a framework should be specific to environment and sustainability, rather than use generalised terms and ideas.

- Third, it should reflect the nature of sustainability problems, especially prime attributes of these problems such as uncertainty and systemic causes.

- Fourth, it should not only identify the elements ("stages") of the policy process, but also identify key principles for policy-making that apply to most or all policy-related activities.

- Fifth, it should emphasise strongly the preconditions of environment and sustainability policy (what comes before a "policy") and the requirements for learning from policy experiments (what comes after).

- Finally, it should refer to the deeper institutional settings that influence policy processes. The next section presents a framework which, although not inconsistent with the policy literature and other models such as those discussed above, attempts to fulfil these criteria.

A framework for policy description, analysis and prescription

We can first identify the basic stages of the policy-making process, in an even more summarised form than the model in Table 4.1. In Table 4.2, four stages are identified and explained, and these form the basic structure of our framework. In Table 4.2, these four stages are equated, where applicable, to the stages identified in the two models considered above.

Table 4.2: Towards a framework – basic stages in the policy process[1]

Stage in the policy process	Equivalent stages from Table 4.1	Equivalent stages from Figure 4.1
1. *Problem-framing*: where the policy community and general community debate issues, gather information, and arrive at a construction of the policy problem.	1	1-2, 4-6
2. *Policy-framing*: where guiding principles are identified, a policy position developed, and policy goals defined.	2-3	5-6
3. *Implementation*: where policy instruments are selected, resources allocated, communication and enforcement activities undertaken, and monitoring mechanisms established.	3-4	3, 7
4. *Monitoring and evaluation*: where ongoing monitoring and evaluation are undertaken to enable learning and enhance performance.	5	8

The identification of four basic stages is only of minimal use and more detail is required. Figure 4.2 sets out more specific elements under each stage, to a level of detail suited to policy description, analysis or prescription, and specific to environment and sustainability. Table 4.3 gives a fuller description of each element, and this is extended a little below and more so in later chapters. Also in

---

[1]   See Figure 4.2 and Table 4.3.

Figure 4.2 and Table 4.3, general elements are identified that should inform policy activities undertaken at different stages of the policy process and in association with specific elements. Taken together, these stages, elements and cyclic interconnections comprise the policy framework that is expanded on in subsequent chapters. The subsequent chapters that deal with each stage are identified in Figure 4.2 and Table 4.3 below.

**Figure 4.2: Summary framework for
analysis and prescription of environment and sustainability policy**

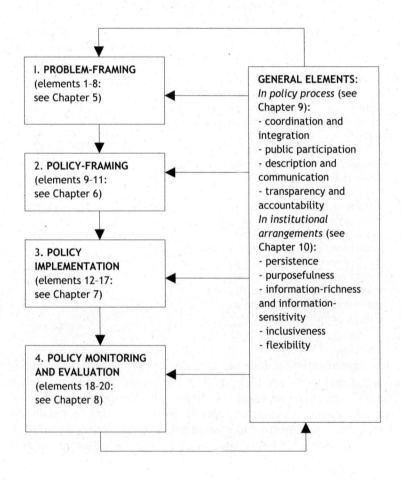

Table 4.3: Detail of framework for analysis and prescription of environmental and sustainability policy

Problem-framing (*Chapter 5*)

1. Discussion and identification of relevant social goals
2. Identification and monitoring of topicality (public concern)
3. Monitoring of natural and human systems and their interactions
4. Identification of problematic environmental or human change or degradation
5. Isolation of proximate and underlying causes of change or degradation
6. Assessment of risk, uncertainty and ignorance
7. Assessment of existing policy and institutional settings
8. Definition (framing and scaling) of policy problems

Policy-framing (*Chapter 6*)

9. Development of guiding policy principles
10. Construction of general policy statement (avowal of intent)
11. Definition of measurable policy goals

Policy implementation (*Chapter 7*)

12. Selection of policy instruments/options
13. Planning of implementation
14. Planning of communication, education, information strategies
15. Provision of statutory, institutional and resourcing requirements
16. Establishment of enforcement/compliance mechanisms
17. Establishment of policy monitoring mechanisms

Policy monitoring and evaluation (*Chapter 8*)

18. Ongoing policy monitoring and routine data capture
19. Mandated evaluation and review process
20. Extension, adaptation or cessation of policy and/or goals

---

General elements, throughout policy and institutional systems

In policy processes (*Chapter 9*):

- Policy coordination and integration (across and within policy fields)
- Public participation and stakeholder involvement
- Transparency, accountability and openness
- Adequate communication mechanisms (multi-directional, democratically structured)

Institutional arrangements (*Chapter 10*):

- Persistence over time
- Purposefulness via mandate and goals
- Information-richness and -sensitivity, including gathering, use and ownership
- Inclusiveness in policy formulation and implementation
- Flexibility, through evaluation, experimentation and learning

The elements in summary

The *problem-framing* stage of the policy process in the framework is more detailed than in most models of the policy cycle, reflecting the particularly contested and complex nature of sustainability problems, and the need to define problems with considerable care. It contains eight elements described further in Chapter 5.

Element 1. *Discussion and identification of relevant social goals.* Sustainability is a higher-order social goal comprising a suite of interconnected issues and problems, poorly understood and involving contested values, and of relevance to all groups in society. As such, it is expectable and proper that widespread social debate over the nature of the problem and appropriate solutions will take place, and policy processes should be sensitive to and connected with such debates.

Element 2. *Identification and monitoring of topicality (public concern).* Within these social debates, particular trends of opinions and areas of stronger or weaker understanding may be evident. Knowledge of these are of great relevance to policy processes, so that policy can benefit from community knowledge, that the direction of policy can be understood by the broader population, and/or that policy interventions can influence public understanding.

Element 3. *Monitoring of natural and human systems and their interactions.* Sustainability issues arise at the intersection of natural and human systems, and thus the best possible understanding of the state of natural systems and human systems, and of human interventions in and impacts on human systems, is a precondition to effective policy responses.

Element 4. *Identification of problematic environmental or human change, or degradation.* From such a knowledge base in close monitoring of natural-human system interactions will emerge the identification of undesirable change or degradation of human or natural systems (a sustainability issue) that requires a policy response, or a positive change that may be enhanced.

Element 5. *Isolation of proximate and underlying causes of change or degradation.* To translate the issue identified in element 4 into a problem suited to finding a solution, the causes of the change or degradation must be isolated. In sustainability, the difference between proximate (direct) and underlying (indirect) causes is important in terms of defining the target of a policy intervention.

Element 6. *Assessment of risk, uncertainty and ignorance.* Even given intensive research, close monitoring and high quality information and communication systems, sustainability problems involve risks, uncertainties and ignorance of various degrees and kinds, which must be identified and accounted for when framing policy problems and interventions.

Element 7. *Assessment of existing policy and institutional settings.* Policy and institutional measures for sustainability attempt to change the behaviours of individuals, households, firms or organisations, which are determined by a complex array of incentives, rules and norms, many of which are set or at least influenced by non-environment or sustainability policies and institutions. These other settings (for example, tax policy, economic incentives, property rights, social norms, and so on) must be assessed for their bearing on either the relevant behaviours, or on the planned policy intervention.

Element 8. *Definition (framing and scaling) of policy problems.* Only once elements 1–7 have been attended to can policy problem/s be defined in a manner suitable for the next stage: policy-framing (and, policy problems will continue to be defined and refined as attention progresses around the policy cycle)

The *policy-framing* stage is much less detailed, reflecting the concentration in this discussion on what comes before and after the "policy", but also the fact that many considerations of what should be in the policy are discussed as discrete elements above and below (see Chapter 6).

Element 9. *Development of guiding policy principles.* Policy design will be guided by both high level and more pragmatic principles, reflecting the position taken on sustainability (for example, precaution, policy integration, and so on) and other concerns (for example, equity, efficiency, and so on). While these may be assumed to always be applied, in the case of a complex, new social goal such as sustainability explicit statement of policy principles is desirable.

Element 10. *Construction of general policy statement (avowal of intent)*. This is the most obvious stage of the policy process, where a government, often in concert with other players, issues a policy statement, recognising a problem and setting out the direction of intended action (usually with appropriate fanfare and publicity).

Element 11. *Definition of measurable policy goals*. As part of the policy statement, but crucially important and worthy of separate identification, policy goals or targets are required. Often these are vague, but it is desirable that there are core parts of the goal set that are measurable, so that later monitoring, evaluation and learning is possible.

The *policy implementation* stage is also more detailed than is usual in policy cycle models. This reflects the importance of policy implementation in any domain, and because it is necessary to delineate the different parts of implementation as clearly as possible, as it is too often the case that one or more implementation tasks remain overlooked (Chapter 7).

Element 12. *Selection of policy instruments/options*. This element involves the selection of the "tools" or policy instruments that will be used to achieve the policy goals (such as taxes, education campaigns, regulation, and so on).

Element 13. *Planning of implementation*. Implementation is a multi-component exercise where one missing or inadequate element can damage the prospects for success, and this recommends comprehensive scheduling of implementation activities.

Element 14. *Planning of communication, education and information strategies*. Policy is an information-rich activity and communication is central to policy success, especially in a domain where the willing, or at least informed, participation of multiple stakeholders is required, and this necessitates differentiated and often intensive communication.

Element 15. *Provision of statutory, institutional and resourcing requirements*. Change is never cost-free, and sustained policy implementation (and monitoring and evaluation) is often resource intensive. Resources are most often thought of as financial, but human, informational, institutional and legal resources are just as important.

Element 16. *Establishment of enforcement / compliance mechanisms.* Many policy instruments (not just regulations) will require some form of enforcement and assurance of compliance during the implementation phase, in turn requiring forward planning of such mechanisms and allocation of appropriate resources.

Element 17. *Establishment of policy monitoring mechanisms.* Rather than leave this until the next stage, the inclusion of this element as part of implementation emphasises that policy monitoring measures should be designed, established and resourced at an early stage rather than being overlooked and possibly forgotten.

The *policy monitoring and evaluation* stage is imperative as it provides an opportunity to learn from policy interventions. The monitoring and evaluation stage contains three elements detailed further in Chapter 8.

Element 18. *Ongoing policy monitoring and routine data capture.* Having established provision for monitoring, these activities will have to be regularly undertaken, especially the routine capture of information required for later evaluation.

Element 19. *Mandated evaluation and review process.* The information gathered through element 18 at some set time will be utilised to assess the success or otherwise of the policy program or instrument, by an identified, responsible individual or organisation.

Element 20. *Extension, adaptation or cessation of policy and/or goals.* On the basis of evaluation and review, the policy intervention may be cancelled, altered or intensified, and the policy problem may be redefined, linking back to the problem-framing stage of the policy process.

General elements

In addressing all the above elements across the four stages, the general elements identified in Figure 4.2 and detailed in Chapters 9 and 10 need to be addressed, reflecting not only the nature of sustainability problems but also good policy practice and the ideals of participatory democracy.

Policy coordination and integration (across and within policy fields). The central logic of sustainability – the integration of environmental, social and economic considerations – is relevant during all stages of the policy process, and is applicable to undertaking many of the elements above.

Public participation and stakeholder involvement. All stages and most elements will have some form and level of broader public involvement in addition to the more immediate policy network and policy community, to be achieved through a wide variety of participatory measures.

Transparency, accountability and openness. In keeping with general standards of modern governance and public administration, and with democratic expectations, transparency and public accountability are required during all elements.

Adequate communication mechanisms (multi-directional, democratically structured). As is emphasised by element 14, comprehensive communication is essential to sustainability policy, but is relevant to all elements.

The general elements necessary to inform organisational and institutional settings that determine the nature of policy processes are those identified in Chapter 2 and explored further in Chapter 10: persistence over time; purposefulness, via mandate and goals; information-richness and information-sensitivity, in terms of gathering, use and wide ownership; inclusiveness in policy formulation and implementation; and flexibility, through evaluation, experimentation and learning.

All these elements are further detailed in Chapters 5–10, and in this chapter it remains only to discuss the ways in which the framework can be utilised, and the qualifications attached to its use.

Using the framework:
The value of checklists

In using the framework it must again be emphasised that it is not a model of how policy is or even how it should be made. It is a guide and an ideal. In a specific policy context, some elements may be far more important than others, and some may not need to be separately undertaken, having already been fulfilled in a previous or concurrent exercise. The stages and specific elements do not represent a linear sequence, nor indeed even a repeatable and predictable cycle. Although cyclic in its structure (see Figure 4.2), policy actors will enter the process at various stages. Different elements will often be addressed in combination rather than in sequence, and there is a certain amount of overlap and redundancy across the range of elements. That redundancy is necessary, given the fact that far too often what appear to be obvious and common sense elements have in fact been forgotten or only scantily observed in practice. While termed a "framework", in practical terms it can be considered a *checklist*, utilised so that things that should be done indeed get done. Checklists are useful in many endeavours, from planning a journey to doing the shopping, and the principle holds for policy-making as well.

The three uses of the framework are descriptive, analytical and prescriptive. Description of a policy process can be aided simply by the identification of the elements in the framework – a language to enable putting names to the parts of a complex pheno-menon. Analysis of a policy process can be similarly aided by these labels, and by the structure of the framework as a cyclic, inter-connected description of policy-making. The framework can aid prescription of new or better policy processes by serving to remind us of the elements that should be included in a comprehensive policy effort.

The framework is not necessarily better than others available, including the two discussed earlier in this chapter, and indeed it is more awkward due to its complexity. However, it is designed specifically for environment and sustainability, and if all the elements are accounted for and addressed, then the chances of policy success will be higher, and the ability to learn from policy efforts so as to improve capacities will be enhanced.

Knowledge and policy processes

A final comment on the framework concerns the issue of *who has what knowledge* that could usefully inform environment and sustainability policy. It is apparent that sustainability policy is not simply a matter for government agencies only, or even for a policy network including a few specialists from outside government as well. This brief discussion emphasises the interdisciplinary and integrative nature of environment and sustainability policy (attribute 15, Table 3.2). The focus here is on the role of different knowledge systems – formal and informal or traditional – rather than on how community knowledge can be incorporated into policy (see Chapter 9) or integrating environmental, social and economic policy (Chapter 10). The precise mix of information, skills and knowledge required will depend greatly on specific contexts, but the following examples for each stage of the policy process serve to illustrate:

1. *Problem-framing.* The discussion and clarification of policy problems invites the specialist capacities of a great many formal *disciplines and professions.* For example, social debate and topicality (elements 1–2) suggest political science, sociology and law, while elements 3–5 require natural sciences such as ecology, hydrology and atmospheric chemistry, depending on the issue being considered. Elements 5 and 6 (identifying causes and uncertainty) require a range of specialist forms of knowledge, while policy assessment and problem definition (elements 7–8) bring public policy and public administration to the fore. For most elements, *other knowledge systems* (community, industry, Indigenous, and so on) are necessary inputs, on par with specialist knowledge, such as for the elements of social debate, topicality, and identification of causes, uncertainty, countervailing policy settings and policy problems.

2. *Policy-framing.* This stage is more the domain of the policy-oriented social sciences (public policy, law, economics, and so on) than other stages, although natural science input is very necessary especially for defining policy goals (element 11). Clearly, the input of knowledge and perspective from outside of both government and formal disciplines is central to developing guiding policy principles and policy goals.

3. *Policy implementation.* The requisite knowledge inputs in this stage are highly variable across elements and across different policy instruments and implementation contexts. A mix of social and natural science disciplines will always be required, and with many

policy instruments (for example, community-based, market, self-regulatory), community or industry knowledge will be crucial. The instruments chosen will have a strong influence – market instruments require economic, commercial and sociological expertise; statutory approaches require lawyers; educative instruments require expertise in communication and education; and so on.

4. *Policy monitoring and evaluation.* Again, depending on the instruments and context, knowledge requirements vary. However, it will usually be the case that environmental monitoring (elements 3–4) will connect strongly to this stage, requiring natural science expertise as well as the social science and administrative expertise necessary to monitor and assess the effectiveness of policy. Specific policy evaluation expertise is also relevant. Given the intent of policy interventions to change behaviour, the perspective of stakeholders (individuals, firms, households, communities) is necessary to evaluation.

Across the stages and the range of substantive issues, we can see a role for many disciplines and professions and other knowledge systems outside of government and the formal disciplines and professions. It is apparent that there is no stage or even specific element where one form of knowledge can believably claim exclusive or even dominant expertise over others. This emphasises a distinctive feature of the framework presented here, in that its focus is less fully on government than many other constructions of the policy process. This is appropriate in modern societies, and particularly suited to environment and sustainability as a policy domain that affects all sectors of society. It is also apparent that the precise mix and emphasis of knowledge and skills required will vary with problems, issues and contexts, instructing those responsible for designing a policy process to carefully consider who is included and excluded.

This challenges the "silo" nature of disciplines and professions, and the trend to increasing reductionism and specialisation in knowledge production and application. Highly specialist and separate areas of knowledge are absolutely needed to handle sustainability – to know what the problems are and how to respond. Indeed, it is widely accepted that much more specialist knowledge is needed. But also needed is greater *interdisciplinary capacity* in research and in applied policy and community settings to enable more integrative approaches. If many disciplines are required, as is made apparent above, then they have to be able to understand each other. Beyond simple mutual understanding, many policy problems in sustainability demand integrated knowledge, especially across the natural and social science domains, and this sort of approach is being explored through interdisciplines such as ecological economics and others (see Barnett et al 2003). One way of exploring interdisciplinary interactions in a practical vein is via an explicit focus on policy problems, using a framework such as that above to identify the full range of knowledge input required (Dovers 2003).

The rest of the book

The interdisciplinary nature of environment and sustainability policy, and other arguments made in Chapters 1–4, will keep emerging as we move through the book. The framework now becomes our structuring device, with the next four chapters covering the four stages of the policy process, and the last two discussing general elements. Chapter 5 is about the most integrative and interdisciplinary of all the four stages: framing the problems that policy will then try and deal with.

PART II

CHECKLISTS AND FRAMEWORKS FOR POLICY ANALYSIS

Chapter 5

PROBLEM-FRAMING

STAGE I: Problem-framing

Element 1:   Debating social goals
Element 2:   Monitoring topicality
Element 3:   Monitoring natural–human systems
Element 4:   Identifying problematic change
Element 5:   Identifying proximate and underlying causes
Element 6:   Assessing uncertainty and risk
Element 7:   Assessing the policy environment
Element 8:   Defining policy problems

This chapter deals with the first stage of the policy cycle, problem-framing, from element 1 (social debate) through to element 8 (problem definition). As with subsequent chapters, space permits only introductory descriptions and presentation of broad guiding frameworks and concepts. The aim for each element is to expose associated challenges and tasks, to provide ways forward beyond the summary description and framework of policy processes established in Chapter 4. For any policy problem faced, there remains the task of operationalising these ideas in specific contexts. In Chapters 9–10, the general elements for policy processes and institutional arrangements in the framework are further explored. Nevertheless, in this and subsequent chapters, these elements will be touched on to indicate parts of the policy process where issues such as inclusiveness, information and transparency are especially relevant.

Element 1: Sustainability as social goal, and the nature of debate

Sustainability and its constituent issues are characterised by uncertainty and multiple values. Uncertainty, even when addressable through specialised research, is a cause of social contest and debate (see element 6). So are multiple values residing in an object of common interest. To explore this, the following defines common values associated with biodiversity, wildlife or ecosystems, which an be translated to other environmental assets, and to all of which significant uncertainty attaches (these categories are not mutually exclusive nor are they cleanly separable):

- *Direct utilitarian values* of immediate consumptive benefit to humans, such as timber, food, medicinal plants and other extractable resources.

- *Indirect utilitarian values,* such as prevention of erosion, native insects pollinating crops, or water from forested catchments.

- *Recreation and amenity value,* either for on-site use or as scenic resources (this category combines elements of both direct and indirect utilitarian values).

- *Scientific and educational value,* or, nature as a resource for scientific discovery and knowledge generation (this often leads to recognition of other values).

- *Existence value,* the recognition of innate value and the right of (usually living) elements of the natural world to exist independent of any use to humans.[1]

- *Option or future value,* maintained in the face of uncertainty and thus of the need to preserve options for use by future generations.

Arguments over and decisions trading off such values and benefits are the stock-in-trade of resource and environmental policy and management. Different values produce different expectations for use and that produces conflict – the stuff of politics. Lee's (1993) definition of politics as "bounded conflict" is apposite – the challenge is to constructively (not constrictively) bound inevitable conflict so as to move forward in an agreed direction.

Not surprisingly, societies have not yet worked through sustainability problems to the extent of agreement on what sustainable use of the environment is, and so sustainability is a focus of social debate. The failure to recognise this in policy processes may result in ignoring important value positions, and concealing them behind assumptions that consensus and agreement regarding policy directions have been achieved. Pretending that policy decisions are

---

[1]   This raises the issue of anthropocentric (human-centred) versus non-anthropocentric values, and the associated philosophical debate about whether existence values are also anthropocentric given they express a human ethical stance or preference.

value-free and not political will usually reduce the prospects for policy success, as value conflicts will re-emerge. The desire of governments to "make issues go away" and achieve instant policy gratification by glossing over value conflicts is at once understandable and unfortunate.

How can we link purposeful policy formulation to an ongoing social debate about the nature of sustainability, and of human-environment relationships? Simply recognising the political nature of significant problems and responses in environment and sustainability is one way, and is why this element of the policy framework is identified. Open recognition that sustainability is a higher order social goal and represents a generational-scale challenge, and therefore that policy and institutional responses are contingent and need to evolve, is another. So is understanding that any worthwhile policy intervention is meant to cause significant behaviour change in society, and that behaviours are deeply embedded in the way people live and henceforth are not variables to be adjusted in an instrumental fashion without wide discussion. The ways in which sustainability has been characterised in Chapters 1 and 3, and how policy is viewed as cyclic and adaptive in Chapter 4, support these orientations.

In more practical terms, there are many options. Significant policy and institutional change is closely interdependent with normative change in the population. Processes to drive institutional change need to be connected to normative debate in society so that directions are not adopted that conflict with values held by significant parts of the community, and are thus not politically viable. This is discussed further in Chapter 10. At a finer resolution, ensuring that policy directions are formulated subsequent to the engagement of the policy community and general public takes time and effort, but increases the chances of recognition of multiple values, development of common understanding and agreement on necessary responses. The participatory policy designs introduced in Chapter 9 offer means to such engagement. Important in this first stage of the policy cycle, and not always clearly articulated, is recognition of what constitutes an exercise of problem-framing. The identification in the policy framework used here of seven elements prior to the definition of a policy problem (most models have only one) underlines the crucial nature of this phase and assists in designing a policy process that allows wide discussion.

A final requirement on the part of individuals and agencies responsible for or capable of establishing opportunities for social debate around sustainability is an awareness of what things are held to be important and how they are understood in the community (element 2).

Element 2: Monitoring topicality

If policy is to be responsive to the values and understanding of issues in society, and if policy interventions are to be effective in the sense of not attracting widespread criticism or non-compliance, then policy networks and actors need to have a good idea of what the community thinks about sustainability problems. At one level, this is both obvious and common practice – governments use opinion polls and other mechanisms to gauge public opinion. That is normal and necessary, but here the emphasis is on a deeper understanding beyond simply what set of issues or priority order of issues the different segments of the public perceive as important, toward an understanding of what information and knowledge shapes those priorities and how judgments on one matter are made relative to other issues. Simple opinion polling has its merits. But superficial opinions may not inform policy very well, and a reliance on such information entails dangers of populist and reactive policy approaches aimed at near-term political advantage.

To inform problem-framing and later policy-framing and implementation, understanding needs to extend to: why people perceive an issue as important; on the basis of what knowledge and information they make that judgment (including cause and effect relationships); how they would frame the issue as a policy problem; what policy responses they believe are appropriate; and the extent to which they perceive connections between problems. Understanding of this across the general population (or a sample thereof), perhaps by the usual major demographic categories of age, employment type, jurisdiction, and so on will be valuable information. However, in a policy sense, such understanding will need to be gained across finer resolution subsets of the population, different issues, geographical regions, and over time to capture shifts in perceptions.

This all suggests a substantial effort in gauging topicality and public perceptions, and it is true that such an undertaking will rarely be trivial. However, the effort expended should be commensurate with the scale of the issue, and a range of approaches exist to choose from (see Chapter 9). These include: qualitative surveys of samples of the population; focus groups and similar structured discussions; utilisation of the existing knowledge of non government or community organisations; advisory groups comprising representatives of key interest groups; or deliberative methods such as citizens' juries.

Public perceptions, agendas and problem definitions often conflict with those of government or of "experts". Some experts are liable to either reject different community opinions outright as uninformed and wrong, or believe that straightforward education is the answer (getting the public to think right). In some cases of strong scientific consensus and serious problems, the latter response might be valid, but there are two weaknesses in such responses. First, the experts might be wrong and the public right, or at least capable of correcting expert judgments. That possibility is a prime reason for community-based approaches to environmental management. Also, different "experts" may have contrasting views. Second, even if the public is "wrong" or significantly misunderstands some environmental issue, public opinion is nonetheless crucially relevant. In risk management, there used to be very different validity attached to *perceived* and *actual* risk, as defined by the community and experts respectively. It is now appreciated that a strongly "perceived" risk or phenomenon is, in the practical world of policy and politics, as real and influential as any number of expert studies and cannot be ignored.

A final consideration relevant to topicality is the media, which has a major influence in public debates. The media can be useful as a communication mechanism between government and community, and between science and the community, but it can also be a barrier. Often, but not always, the popular media is unsuited as a means of communicating or discussing matters that are complex and/or long term in nature. The uses and abuses of the media in policy debates is a major topic that cannot be dealt with here, and most policy agencies recognise the importance of the media and have specialised staff and processes for media engagement. Often in the case of environment and sustainability, it is members of epistemic communities such as scientists who have the greatest difficulty in engaging fruitfully with the media. This is often the result of a belief that the knowledge they possess is a priority and interesting to others, and a lack of understanding of the limits of the media to handle complexity and uncertainty.

Elements 3-4: Monitoring change in natural and human systems

It would be difficult to argue against the proposition that close monitoring of the state and functioning of natural systems, and of human impacts on those systems, is crucial to responding to sustainability problems. Most official policy statements stress the importance of good information and sound science, and environment groups argue for more investment in this area and scientists do so even more strongly. Without close monitoring we cannot detect changes in the environment or human use of it that present problems or opportunities, thus allowing the definition of policy problems that require and are amenable to policy interventions. Poor information equals poor policy. We face massive information gaps, even though much has been done to address these in recent years, in areas such as climate change, biodiversity and ocean management.

Long-term environmental research and monitoring (LTERM) are a major determinant of policy agendas, and discoveries or confirmations of problems from LTERM have shifted agendas quickly at times. The time from scientific recognition of a phenomenon to definition of a policy problem and policy response can be quite swift, at least as measured in institutional time scales. The rise of climate change as a paramount issue from the early 1980s when it was barely on the political agenda through to the UN Framework Convention on Climate Change in 1992 is a case in point. Another example is the serendipitous recognition of the issue of ozone depletion. Monitoring needs to be *basic* in nature, recognising that, given temporal scale, complexity and uncertainty as problem attributes, we cannot rely on monitoring programs that address only issues currently on the agenda. Unexpected changes are likely and may not be detected by narrow or short-term monitoring. Yet a case for such narrowing of monitoring to only those "issues that matter" is commonly argued on the basis of resource constraints and efficiency. Monitoring must be broadly scoped across environmental issues and sectors to capture unexpected change, consistent with a proactive (precautionary) and adaptive policy style.

Another information strategy is the use of summary or composite indicators for use in policy-making, to reduce the information set to a tractable level, and to extract meaning from limited data.[2] Indicators can be highly useful, but are defined in their validity and usefulness by the more detailed and specific data that underpins them.

However, it is the case that chronic under-investment in information gathering, and especially long-term research and monitoring, is common. There are reasons for this – ongoing environmental monitoring, as opposed to innovative research, entails little reward for scientists in terms of reputation, funding or publications. Monitoring also has few political rewards: it is not newsworthy and often stretches beyond the time scales of electoral terms or even political tenures. Monitoring of human interactions with the environment, unless there are traded goods and services involved, is similarly unsupported by scientific or political incentives.

Thus, there is a clear case for policy processes to be based on comprehensive and long-term monitoring programs. However, there will always be limits to what can be afforded, and policy and decisions will still be made in the face of insufficient information and pervasive uncertainty. Therefore, it is important to recognise the limits of monitoring and the information supporting policy decisions, so that: (a) residual uncertainties can be accurately described and handled (element 6); and (b) later policy monitoring and evaluation can take uncertainty and missing data into account.[3]

A final consideration regarding this element is who undertakes monitoring. As noted above, researchers lack incentives to engage in monitoring, and resources for long-term programs are scarce. Policy agencies rarely have the on-ground capacity or skills for monitoring, and even land management agencies have difficulty justifying or implementing ongoing monitoring programs. More innovative approaches to monitoring have emerged recently – especially the use of community-based monitoring programs (see Chapter 9) – which require resolution of issues of data validity, continuity of programs, and technical and financial support from government. The other trend in recent decades in monitoring is remote sensing (satellite images, unmanned data recorders, and so on), which has revolutionised data gathering in some fields but raises issues of the limits of inference from incomplete data sets and the ownership and dissemination of data. Whatever the sources or mix of sources, a central capacity is always required for quality

---

2   The journal *Ecological Indicators* is a useful source of detail on this topic.
3   Fuller arguments for this claim, and of the need for long-term monitoring, are given in Dovers (2001).

control, resourcing, continuity and dissemination. Given the collective and long-term nature of environmental problems and information, some significant component of this central or coordinating capacity must be the responsibility of the public sector.

Element 5: Identify proximate and underlying causes

A feature of the move from traditional, narrow environmental management to the recent era of integrated environmental management and sustainability has been the shift from "end-of-pipe" or reactive responses towards "upstream" policy interventions that address root causes. This attends the important problem attribute of systemic causes (Chapter 3), and is the justification for the policy instrument choice criterion explained in Chapter 7 of a corrective versus antidotal focus. For most environment and sustainability problems, there will be one or a few *proximate* or direct causes, and generally a greater number of *underlying* or indirect causes. Human behaviours are driven by multiple factors and policy interventions to change behaviours need to address those drivers. To illustrate, Table 5.1 sets out three examples of problems, simply stated, along with the proximate cause and some selected underlying causes.

These are simple examples, but they serve the purpose of emphasising that different causes invite the use of different policy styles and instruments. For example, in the case of problem 1 in Table 5.1, the proximate cause (clearance by farmers) invites a regulatory approach – simply banning clearing in sensitive areas. That approach provides a disincentive to clearing but does not address the underlying causes that push behaviour towards clearing. Recognition of the underlying causes in this case suggests a more sophisticated mix of policy instruments to address the various causes, comprising educative, taxation and regulatory approaches.

There are two general categories of indirect causes. The first are those determined by policy settings, often formulated in other policy domains, and these should be quickly amenable to adjustment in the near term (see element 7 below). The second are causes more deeply embedded in cultural attitudes, knowledge systems or institutional arrangements, that are more difficult policy targets (see Chapter 10).

Table 5.1: Examples of proximate and underlying causes

Problem	Proximate cause (example)	Underlying causes (selected)
1. Remnant vegetation loss in farmland, leading to wildlife loss and salinity	Clearance by landholders to create pasture resource	Economic pressure from non-viable property size and/or commodity price decline. Increased demand due to regional industry development policy investments in local feedlot capacity. Tax deductions against clearing costs. Lack of understanding of biodiversity or hydrological value of native vegetation.
2. Pressure to build new water storage reservoir, with environmental impacts	Increasing per capita water use in households	Unsuitable urban design. Increasing house size plus decreasing persons/household. Proliferation of water-intensive consumer goods (eg spas, swimming pools). High cost of efficient versus inefficient water-using technologies.
3. Climate change	Increasing per capita fossil fuel consumption	Prices for carbon rich energy sources that do not reflect environmental or social costs. Over-investment in road system, under-investment in public transport. Urban planning encouraging private vehicles. Subsidies and price reductions to bulk electricity users. Cost of (unsubsidised) alternative fuels and efficiency measures.

Element 6: Assess ignorance, uncertainty and risk

Uncertainty is a key attribute of policy problems in environment and sustainability. Indeed, if there was little uncertainty attached to issues such as climate change, biodiversity, water resource management or basic human needs, they would not be issues. Uncertainty characterises many other policy problems; however the sources and forms of uncertainty in environment and sustainability are acute and particular to the domain. Yet sound conceptualisation of uncertainty and clear choices about how to handle it are not always apparent. To paraphrase the attribute description in Chapter 3, while understanding of natural systems and the implications of human interventions in them has improved, poor information, risks and uncertainties remain highly problematic for policy and management and for public debate. Common *sources of uncertainty* in environment and sustainability are: the state of the environment and of natural resources and processes; the extent of human use and impacts on the environment; the long-term implications of those impacts; and the effectiveness of policy and management strategies. Moreover, natural systems, especially those subject to human utilisation and management, change in constant and unpredictable ways, and thus are very often "moving targets" in terms of both scientific and policy understanding.

More research and monitoring, and well-structured public debate, (see elements 2–5, and Chapter 9) are strategies for *reducing uncertainty*, but rarely will uncertainty be fully addressed. *Residual uncertainty* will always exist and policy and decision-making needs to handle uncertainty in effective and accountable ways. The main policy principle in this regard is the precautionary principle, which is stated in much international and national policy and law. A typical definition of the principle is:

> *Where there are threats of serious or irreversible environmental damage, lack of full scientific certainty should not be used as a reason for postponing measures to prevent environmental degradation.*

The precautionary principle recognises uncertainty and the need to make decisions under conditions of uncertainty, and recommends a more proactive approach; that is, not waiting for absolute proof before acting to protect the environment. The precautionary principle is a codification of changing societal values: we used not to care much about the environment, whereas now we do and should act accordingly. What is not simple is how to understand uncertainty in different situations, and how to identify appropriate ways of informing policy and decision-making; that is, operationalising the precautionary principle. To offer guidance the following discusses the nature of uncertainty, the implications of not dealing with uncertainty explicitly, how different knowledge systems handle uncertainty, and what policy support approaches exist.[4]

Uncertainty is conceptualised and handled very differently across disciplines, political cultures and informal knowledge systems. Western scientific and decision-making traditions tend to define uncertainty as something that can be reduced by knowledge gathering and is best handled through quantitative methods (usually probabilistic). This is a valid and useful approach, but in policy-making contexts many forms and degrees of uncertainty exist. An initial set of definitions follows (drawing on Dovers and Handmer 1995; Wynne 1992):[5]

- *Risk*, where believable probability distributions can be assigned to possible outcomes (that is, we know the odds). For example, the likely impacts on well-researched aquatic species of the release of a known chemical into a stream.

- *Uncertainty*, where the direction of change is known, but precision in predicting the scale or probability of impacts is not possible (for example, the current scientific consensus with climate change).

- *Ignorance*, where not even the broad directions of change are known, and where thresholds and surprises are understood as likely (for example, local impacts of climate change).

An important dimension of uncertainty for policy is proposed by Wynne (1992) – that uncertainty and ignorance will change and increase if policy or technological commitments are made on the basis of knowledge that is imperfect. Also crucial is recognition that uncertainty does not simply exist out there in the environment, but is produced in human systems – uncertainty is socially constructed and politically negotiated. Attention must be paid to scientific uncertainties in environment and sustainability, but to other forms as well. This is made clear in Smithson's (1989) *taxonomy of ignorance*, which begins with a division between that which we ignore (irrelevance) and that which we do not know (error), an abbreviated form of which follows:

---

[4]   Also problematic in the precautionary principle is the definition of "serious or irreversible', which will be judged quite differently across diverse policy actors. Elements 2–5 above and Chapters 9 and 10 discuss this.

[5]   Although we will recognise variants of uncertainty here, that term will be used as the overall descriptor.

Irrelevance (to ignore):
- untopicality (outside cognitive or intuitive domain)
- undecidability (believed insoluble or not requiring verification)
- taboo (socially enforced ignorance).

Error (to be ignorant of):
- distortion (of knowledge)
  - confusion (distortion in kind via wrongful substitution)
  - inaccuracy (distortion in degree)
- incompleteness (of knowledge)
  - absence (incompleteness in kind)
  - uncertainty (incompleteness in degree)
  - ambiguity (equivocal meanings)
  - probability (risk)
  - vagueness (indescribability).

Smithson's taxonomy is arguably the most rigorous and sophisticated one available, and close consideration of it enables a better understanding of uncertainty. It relegates the most common characterisations in science and policy – scientific uncertainty and probabilistic risk – to the lower levels, indicating that other forms of uncertainty are also important. Put more bluntly, political and policy processes are beset with taboos, equivocation, uneven distribution of knowledge, intentional or unintentional distortion, confusion and so on. More than one form of uncertainty will be evident in one problem context, and different policy actors will be responding to different forms and must be accounted for in policy-making.

Overlooking uncertainty will usually result in (a) policy failure due to incorrect assumptions, and/or (b) the inability to properly understand the causes of policy failure and thus any improvements that should be made. Adaptive policy becomes unlikely. Pervasive uncertainty emphasises the need for close monitoring of policy and management interventions (Chapter 8), and appropriate participation strategies and institutional settings (Chapters 9 and 10). As well as recognising sources and forms of uncertainty, it is necessary to understand and incorporate different responses to uncertainty across the policy community, variations which result from disciplinary or professional as well as economic and psychological perspectives. Politicians and other decision-makers often suppress uncertainty so as to appear decisive and convince others to support them. Other people recognise but downplay risks, in the interests of gaining benefits from proposed economic or other activity. Researchers might stress the need for careful research and information gathering prior to decision-making, whereas members of the community may be very risk-averse if their interests appear to be at stake.

Behind attitudes to uncertainty are different *burdens of proof* that are implicit or explicit in how people judge the need for action or inaction in the face of uncertainty (see Cranor 1999). The pre-cautionary principle suggests a shift in the burden of proof towards environmental protection. In a policy domain with multiple actors, values and sources and forms of uncertainty, transparency over the burdens of proof being brought into a policy debate is essential. Some burdens will be apparent, such as a stated 98 per cent confidence limit in a scientific report, or the difference between "beyond reasonable doubt" and "on the balance of probability" in criminal versus civil law. Others will be less clear, such as the realism of assumptions in economic models, lay judgments of stakeholder groups, or reportage of the media.

Although the above makes handling uncertainty sound highly problematic, there are a range of decision-making and policy support methods that can assist. Some of these are well known, such as risk assessment or use of specialist commissions of inquiry. But the issue of when to use which tool is not clear. Part of the difficulty is that different approaches to decision-making in the face of uncertainty are not differentiated enough. Table 5.2 presents a "toolkit" of techniques and approaches, and organises them within a hierarchy of goals, principles, frameworks and tools. The precautionary principle is often mistakenly understood to instruct us on what decision to make – in fact it instructs us to be careful and to better handle uncertainty. Table 5.2 identifies the precautionary principle, along with adaptive management, as a guiding principle that sits beneath the social goal of sustainability, while the third and fourth rows indicate ways of operationalising such a principle. In Table 5.2, tools and techniques are organised into those relevant to proximate or direct environmental impacts and causes of sustainability, and underlying or indirect ones (see element 5 above).

Various tools will be more suitable in different contexts. In the case of quantifiable direct impacts without too many variables, risk assessment models will be useful; whereas for unquantifiable or highly complex cases, expert judgment and/or a deliberative

Table 5.2: Decision-making hierarchy for the precautionary principle

Level	Components
1. Social goal	Sustainability/sustainable development
2. *Principles* (codified in policies and laws)	Precautionary principle Adaptive management
3. *Frameworks* (through which principles are applied and specific techniques chosen)	Risk management standards (eg Australian Standard 4360) Policy assessment procedures (eg strategic assessment) Others (eg ISO 14000 environmental management series)
4. *Tools and techniques* (selected examples, toolkit to be filled)	a) Proximate or direct causes and impacts: - research and monitoring (focused) - policy monitoring and evaluation - environmental impact assessment - risk assessment - expert judgment - extended cost-benefit analysis - non-market valuation - performance assurance bonds - multi-criteria analysis (deterministic) - mediation, negotiation - small scale deliberative techniques (eg citizens' juries, focus groups) - population viability analysis - regulatory safe minimum standards - court proceedings b) Underlying or indirect causes and impacts: - long-term research and monitoring - policy monitoring and evaluation - strategic environment assessment - sustainability assessment, integrated assessment - strategic risk assessment - expert judgment - mediation, negotiation - multi-criteria analysis (heuristic) - large scale deliberative techniques (eg deliberative polling, consensus conferences) - commissions of inquiry - court proceedings

approach would be more suitable. For indirect causes of a non-urgent nature, research and monitoring is appropriate, but not for more urgent problems where a quicker response is required via expert judgment or a commission of inquiry.

The institutional capacity to employ different approaches to supporting policy decisions in the face of uncertainty across time and problems is an important matter. Often, the mandate and expertise to do so is not evident, and possible remedies to that situation are discussed in Chapter 10.

Element 7: Assess the policy environment

This element follows from the identification of proximate and especially underlying causes at element 5. The essence is that no policy works in isolation. The individual human and organisational behaviours that cause environmental degradation or present opportunities for improvement are shaped by multiple factors, including – whether directly or indirectly – other policy settings. These policy settings may be targeting sustainability, or more often they will be social or economic policies that determine patterns of production and consumption and that have unintended consequences for environment and sustainability.[6]

Some simple examples. A policy to reduce private car use and thus pollution through an education campaign is unlikely to be effective if major public investment in road construction and a lack of alternative transport options encourage car use. Or, where grants to encourage installing energy efficiency processes in industry are outweighed by reductions in the price of electricity to bulk consumers produced via competitive restructuring of utilities. In reality, the situation will often be more complex, with multiple influences.

The design of policy interventions should include identification of other policy settings and the incentives or disincentives they create. The point of this element is to identify which influences are either *created by existing policy* or are *amenable to change via reform of existing policy*. Common forms of countervailing policy settings include perverse incentives (for example, subsidies for environmentally damaging behaviours), provision of non-

---

[6] Such unintended consequences are central to the sustainability problem, and to the imperative for policy integration (Chapters 3 and 10).

economic incentives or messages via policy (for example, a non-environmental policy encouraging unsustainable consumption), and regulatory or other barriers to improved environmental performance (for example, burdensome procedures for approving environmental technologies). The identification of such policy settings creates a double opportunity for policy impact, by removing negative factors (the existing, countervailing policy) as well as putting in place a positive factor (a new policy). At least new policy can be better designed if other influences are understood and factored in. Note that some determinants of unsustainable behaviours are not created by countervailing policy settings but by other factors (for example, cultural norms, lack of information, and so on) and need to be defined as a separate class of underlying causes and thus treated differently.

Element 8: Defining policy problems

This element translates elements 1–7 into a tractable statement. Social goals, topicality, scientific information, understanding of causes and the policy environment, and an appreciation of uncertainty, all shape the definition of a policy problem or set of problem/s. Policy *problems* are for solving, while *issues* are for debating. Problem definition often involves reducing larger problems down to a finer scale or into sub-sets that are more suitable for policy attention.

Yet such reduction can serve to lose purchase on the larger social goals and issues by focusing attention only on less significant and disjointed problems. Problem definition is a balance between tractability and clarity of definition ("bite-sized pieces") and continued relevance to the social goal of sustainability and to higher order environmental issues. This requires a conceptualisation and framework that allows three things to occur: definition or *framing*; assessing magnitude or *scaling*; and maintaining connection via a *hierarchy* of suites of problems.

To provide a framework for considering these three aspects, Table 5.3 sets out problem attributes to be used in problem definition, and matching "scale descriptors" that can guide assessing magnitude, followed by a typology of problem types and an example from biodiversity conservation. The attributes in Table 5.3 are those of the general attributes of policy problems in sustainability presented in Table 3.2 most relevant to problem definition.

Table 5.3: Framing and scaling policy problems in sustainability

Problem attributes	Scale descriptors
Problem-framing attributes	
1. Spatial scale of cause or effect	Local – national – regional – global
2. Magnitude of possible impacts: a) on natural systems b) on human systems	Minor – moderate – severe – catastrophic
3. Temporal scale of possible impacts: a) timing/onset b) longevity/persistence	Months to years – years to decades – decades to centuries
4. Reversibility	Easily reversed – difficult – irreversible
5. Measurability of factors and processes	Risk – uncertainty – ignorance (see element 6)
6. Complexity and connectivity	Discrete/linear – multiple feedbacks and linkages
Response-framing attributes	
7. Nature of cause/s	Discrete/simple – multiple – multiple and systemic
8. Relevance to jurisdiction	Beyond jurisdiction – relevant – core responsibility
9. Tractability: a) availability of means b) acceptability of means	a) instruments/processes sufficient – insufficient b) social/political barriers negligible – significant
10. Public concern/topicality a) Level of concern b) Basis of concern	a) low – moderate – high b) widely shared – varied understanding – highly disparate understanding
11. Existence of social/policy goals	Clearly stated – generally stated – absent

Source: Dovers 1995

These attributes are important features of a problem and are divided into those most relevant to problem-framing (the nature of the problem) and to response-framing (what we do about it). The scale descriptors in the second column prompt consideration of relative difficulty.

Applying the framework in Table 5.3 is a matter of judgment and flexibility across specific situations. It is not a blueprint or strict procedure but a way of structuring debate and analysis. A simple hierarchical typology of problem types can emerge from this, once again not a strict categorisation but a useful device, describing relative magnitude as well as allowing recognition of connectivity between higher and lower-order problems:

- *Micro-problems*, where most problem attributes would be placed at the lower or less problematic end of the scales in the second column. These are routine challenges to policy processes – they are spatially and temporally bounded, have limited uncertainty, are addressable through existing processes and familiar instruments, and are not subject to much social debate.

- *Meso-problems*, where most attributes would be placed in the middle range. These problems are difficult, significant and topical, but do not pose systemic threats to current patterns of production and consumption, or overwhelming challenges to existing policy processes, institutions or technologies. This category may also include policy processes or decisions across a suite or type of micro-problem, such as establishing an impact assessment regime for a jurisdiction or a national air quality standards framework.

- *Macro-problems*, where the majority of attributes are in the upper range. These are big, composite sustainability problems stemming from systemic causes – they are multi-faceted and complex, pervaded by uncertainties, dispersed in space and time, highly connected to other problems and pose major threats to natural and human systems. They are beyond the apparent capacity of existing knowledge, policy processes, institutional arrangements and technological capacities, and are subject to intense social debate.

These three categories are loose, and much subjective judgment and discussion would take place around categorising an issue. That is inevitable and the framework provides a basis for making such discussion more constructive by forcing attention on *why a problem is important* or not, rather that simply that someone thinks it is and someone else thinks it is not. Categorising the problem assists in structuring problem definition (see below), and also suggests the sorts of knowledge and processes needed to address different problems.

The three categories match a categorisation of the type of knowledge and science that different global environmental problems demand, developed by Funtowicz and Ravetz (1991). They defined problems according to a high–medium–low scale of two variables, "decision stakes" (equivalent to attributes 1–4 in Table 5.3) and "systems uncertainty" (equivalent to attributes 5–6). They define three approaches: (a) *applied science* or problem-solving, suitable for micro-problems; (b) what they term *professional consultancy* involving multiple inputs and judgments, suitable for meso-problems; and (c) *post-normal science*, suitable for macro-problems. Funtowicz and Ravetz (1991) describe this schema as a heuristic tool and advise against any pretence of quantifying any prioritisation, in a similar vein to the qualification attached to using Table 5.3.

The micro–meso–macro typology is scale-dependent; that is, it can be applied to relative magnitudes of problems across jurisdictional scales (for example, local, provincial, national, and so on). What will be defined as a macro-problem locally (for example, a large development proposal in a small town) may be judged a micro-problem at a higher level of government. Also, the magnitude of a problem changes over time as knowledge is gained, policy instruments are adapted and value expectations in society are reconciled. Ozone depletion was initially a classic macro-problem, but over time as the policy and technological responses were worked out it has become more tractable. Similarly, the creation of a new legislative and management regime in a natural resource sector may be a macro-problem for government and stakeholders initially, but may settle down over time. This maturation of problems while they remain on the agenda is different to shifts in topicality and the disappearance from policy and political agendas of issues for less explicable reasons.

To bring this together, we can use an illustrative example from biodiversity conservation. To continue with the terminology, this example is placed under a fourth problem category – the "meta-problem" or social goal of sustainability:

Meta-problem (social goal): sustainability;
  Macro-problem (selected): conserving biodiversity;
    Meso-problem (selected): biodiversity loss in production forests;
      Micro-problems:
        • lack of protected habitat strips and patches;
        • forest agency objectives not including biodiversity;
        • prescribed fire regime not accounting for wildlife;
        • no monitoring of wildlife impacts of logging;
        • management staff untrained in wildlife management;
        • and so on.

Such a hierarchical problem-framing exercise could be repeated in endless different policy contexts in environment and sustainability. This example serves to illustrate the process and potential for clarity. Problem definition of this kind is an entry point to the next stage of the cycle – policy-framing (Chapter 6).

Chapter 6

POLICY-FRAMING

STAGE II: Policy-framing

Element 9:   Developing guiding principles
Element 10:   Constructing the policy statement
Element 11:   Defining measurable policy goals

This chapter identifies some basic requirements for fulfilling elements 9–11 of the framework: the identification and use of guiding policy principles; content and purpose of the policy statement; and definition of policy goals. The most common manifestation of public policy – the policy statement – is finally discussed here but, in keeping with our emphasis on what comes before and after the statement, the treatment is shorter than for virtually any other element.

Element 9: Guiding principles for environment and sustainability policy

All policy decisions are influenced by a range of imperatives that bear upon different policy actors. These imperatives vary across policy domains, and the influence may be weak or strong and the consideration of them implicit or explicit. Sometimes, the considerations that determined the nature of the policy direction taken will be unclear or unstated, at others times the considerations will be obvious and/or stated. In some policy domains and areas of public administration practice, generic imperatives are stated as *policy principles* to be applied in an explicit fashion. While there are very real limits to how prescriptive such principles can be, the clear expression and application of policy principles has three benefits:

- Specifying the logic and meaning of a social goal in more operational terms, and seeking to ensure that key elements of that logic are considered by actors within a policy network.

- Communicating the meaning of a social goal more widely and usefully to members of a policy community, especially in terms of the justification for policy decisions.

- Enhancing transparency and accountability in policy processes to the broader public.

In mature and familiar policy domains, policy principles often become "background knowledge", or implicit assumptions that are not clearly articulated or are only articulated when a policy decision is questioned. That is less than ideal especially for a social goal or policy problem that is new and must be dealt with across multiple policy sectors. Sustainability and even more familiar environmental problems are relatively recent additions to the policy agenda. Also, decisions will be made across many policy domains, often by policy actors not familiar with sustainability. Thus there is a strong argument for making the core set of principles explicit, not as a set of rigid rules, but to communicate the operational logic of sustainability and to inform and guide policy decisions wherever they are made.

Table 6.1 presents a core set of guiding principles for environmental and especially sustainability policy. The sources for these are: the Rio Declaration (UN 1992) as the core international statement on sustainable development; the attributes of sustainability problems defined in Table 3.2; and principles that have become widely recognised in environmental policy in recent decades. They are also informed by the policy and institutional challenges defined in Chapter 3 and are organised under the headings used in Table 3.3. However, there are core sustainability principles that relate to substantial and material considerations that cannot be sensibly captured under categories that relate to process matters, and these are included in the last row.

The list in Table 6.1 is neither exhaustive or definitive, but captures the essence of what sustainability has come to mean in theory and practice. Other principles may be considered relevant in a given societal or problem context, and it is likely that forcing attention to an iteration such as the one in Table 6.1 will result in the identification of these. Although they flesh out the policy and institutional challenges, all require a finer scale of consideration across different stages and elements of the policy cycle – where this book offers further detail, the relevant Chapter is noted.

Table 6.1: Guiding principles for sustainability policy

Policy and institutional challenge	Guiding principles
1. Long-term policy	Create informational, policy and institutional settings that allow development of longer-term policy mandates and strategies.
	Consider the long-term implications of policy decisions, especially ecological but also social and economic.
	Consider new operational elements of policy processes beyond the time frames normally applicable in the jurisdiction.
2. Inter- and intra-generational equity	Consider long- and near-term equity in decision-making.
	Recognise eradication of poverty as central to sustainability.
	Emphasise equity impacts on disadvantaged or marginalised groups.
3. Global dimensions	Consider regional and global implications of policy decisions for environment and human well-being.
	Ensure domestic policy decisions do not result in outcomes less than specified in international agreements.
	Include sustainability as a priority in development aid policy and in domestic engagement in international policy development.
	Trade and economic policies should not encourage or subsidise unsustainable production or consumption.
4. Policy integration	Policy and project decisions should be subject to an assessment regime to identify and minimise environmental and sustainability impacts (Chapter 10).
	Ensure environmental protection is embedded in economic and development planning from the earliest stages.
	Ensure integration of ecological, social and economic policy through (a) policy processes and institutional settings, and (b) use of policy support techniques (Chapter 10).
	Consider costs and benefits of environmental protection, applying, as appropriate, the principles of user-pays, polluter-pays and/or beneficiary-pays.
	Sustainability policy should be supported by national policy frameworks, legal expression and suitable institutions (Chapter 10).

Policy and institutional challenge	Guiding principles
5. Biodiversity and ecological processes	Express protection of biodiversity and ecological processes as priority goals across all policy sectors.
	Consider the implications of policy decisions for biodiversity and ecological processes, through transparent methods.
6. Information focus	Ensure the maximum possible use, distribution and ownership of information in policy processes.
	Utilise multiple knowledge systems as valid inputs to policy, including formal and informal, expert and community (Chapters 5, 9).
	Enhance connections between information systems and policy processes (Chapters 5, 8).
	Create and maintain broadly focused long-term environmental research and monitoring (Chapter 5).
	Require rigorous monitoring and evaluation of policy and management interventions (Chapter 8).
	Place priority on education for sustainability.
7. Precaution	Require application of the precautionary principle in all decision-making processes (Chapter 5).
	Recognise and consider risks and uncertainties in policy problems and responses (Chapter 5).
	Identify and require transparent use of decision and policy support methods for incorporating uncertainty (Chapter 5).
	Use no-regret options (environmental costs uncertain but benefits apparent therefore neutral social or economic costs justify action).
8. Inter-jurisdictional	Identify aspects of problems that cross political and administrative boundaries, especially those dealt with through separate informational, policy and/or institutional arrangements.
	Establish strategies for inter-jurisdictional coordination of policy through information sharing, joint policy formulation and implementation or institutional reform (Chapter 10).

Policy and institutional challenge	Guiding principles
9. Participation	Identify groups in society likely or possibly interested in and/or affected by decisions ("stakeholders").
	Enable public participation in policy through multiple and flexible means (Chapter 9).
	Ensure transparency and accountability of decision and policy-making processes (Chapter 9).
	Emphasise the participation and empowerment of marginalised groups (the poor, isolated, Indigenous, women, youth).
10. Innovative policy approaches	Require explicit consideration of a full menu of policy approaches and instruments (Chapter 7).
	In selecting instruments, use stated criteria (Chapter 7).
	Encourage and mandate use of and experimentation with non-traditional policy approaches, including information-based, inclusive and market instruments (Chapters 7, 9).
11. Substantive/ material principles	Favour policies that serve to reduce throughputs of materials and energy per unit of social or economic benefit.
	Maintain spare assimilative capacity in environmental sinks, and spare capacity in renewable resource stocks.
	Favour sustainable use of renewable resources over non-renewable resources.
	Ensure rent capture from non-renewable resource use to allow investment in long-term alternatives.

Policy principles are different and should be considered separately from more practical constraints faced in a particular context. For example, the principle of efficiency in expending public resources – getting the best policy outcome per unit of expenditure – applies universally as a fundamental principle of public administration. In a specific policy context, there will be budget or other constraints which limit policy choices: the efficiency principle applies *within* that limit, but should not be used to justify it. The principle of sophisticated policy instrument choice may be constrained, or fully abandoned, in the face of a government's ideological commitment to one or a limited range of instruments (that is different from a rapid but justified narrowing of the instrument menu supported by reference to the problem type). In such a case, responsible members of the policy community should identify that a principle has been compromised and seek to ensure that the nature of instrument choice is recorded so as to inform later evaluation and subsequent consideration of policy change.

Policy principles are not rules, for three reasons. The first is that elected governments and/or members of the policy community with delegated authority will require some flexibility to decide priorities in a given context and their priorities may favour or override some principles. Given that such prioritisation is publicly justified, this is appropriate in the face of highly variable contexts. The second reason is that some principles are in potential conflict and have to be balanced against each other – for example, long-term monitoring versus precautionary (proactive) responses, or equity considerations versus user or polluter pays. This is the same with the criteria for policy instrument choice set out in Chapter 7, some of which are not unexpectedly related to these policy principles. Policy principles express the social goal of sustainability and can inform and guide decisions, but they cannot not make those decisions for us. The third reason is that the relevance of policy principles may well change over the policy cycle, as problems become better understood and policy directions are evaluated and adjusted or as public expectations change.

Furthermore, the principles in Table 6.1 are those expressing the social goal of sustainability and especially the environmental aspects of sustainability. In many policy-making situations, other principles and imperatives will be relevant, expressing other social goals such as near-term economic growth or national security. These principles will be traded off against sustainability when they are in conflict. Indeed, such trading off – or more ideally integration – is a central challenge in sustainability policy discussed in Chapter 10.

Element 10: The policy statement

The most visible part of a policy process is the policy statement, usually in the form of a publicly available document, and this is separated out and discussed as a distinct element here. The policy statement should make policy decisions and directions, including the relevant principles above, a matter of accessible public record. Stage II of the policy cycle – policy-framing – involves a commitment to a course of action, based on the policy problems defined and the policy principles identified as relevant. The cyclic nature of policy becomes problematic here, as the commitment will also include key parts of the policy response expressed through elements 12–17 in Stage III.

However, in the terminology used here, the policy statement is an "avowal of intent" in more general terms, and it is in the nature of democratic politics that governments will issue policy positions or statements. It is also necessary from a communication viewpoint for them to do so. Very simple statements of position, such as those made in an election campaign, are different to the more substantial policy statements under discussion here, which will offer more detail.

An additional difficulty is that rarely will only one "statement" be issued with regard to any significant policy problem – the reality being that a number of related or sequential policy statements will be developed and released. While that complicates matters, the specification below is still relevant as a guide.

To provide guidance for what a policy statement should do, here we can restate the policy framework as content items (Table 6.2). Although somewhat redundant, it remains the case that policy statements do not always reflect a full and apparent policy process, and as the most visible product and communication mechanism (especially for the public and policy actors not closely engaged), another checklist is warranted.

Note that some of the detail of elements 12–17, and perhaps some of the general policy and institutional elements may, understandably, be unclear when a major policy statement is issued. In such cases, this lack of clarity would be addressed by either or both inclusion of the process by which these elements will be addressed and by issuing supplementary statements.

As with other checklists and tools in this book, Table 6.2 must be interpreted and applied across many, variable contexts, and thus the content items are flexible guidelines rather than strict instructions. They do however prompt the inclusion of what comes before and after the "policy" in what is usually the most publicly and politically visible stage of the policy cycle. The key requirement is that a policy statement does not simply communicate the policy decision and direction, but makes clear the basis upon which these have been decided, and how they will be achieved, observed and learned from.

A particular weakness of many policies in environment and sustainability is the statement of policy goals in a manner consistent with later monitoring, evaluation and adaptive learning, to which we now turn.

Table 6.2: Core content of a policy statement

Content item	Explanation
Identify the mandate and authority	Identify the mandate and responsible and/or delegated authorities under which the policy is issued and will be implemented. Describe parts of the policy community consulted and who are supportive.
Identify the problem	Define the policy problem/s addressed, and those not addressed. Identify related policy problems and processes and how these are or are not linked to the policy.
Explain the problem context	Identify the nature, source and limits of information used in formulating the policy. Identify residual and uncertainties.
State the policy direction	Describe overall intent of the policy intervention. State policy goals. Describe the hierarchy of policies, programs and projects. Identify instruments to be used to achieve policy goals.
Detail implementation	Describe implementation plan and timeframe and commitments of financial, human, institutional and statutory resources. Set out communication plan including audiences and timing and form of information outputs. Clarify responsibilities and roles of all parties in implementation.
Describe ongoing activities	Describe policy monitoring and evaluation. Specify information requirements for monitoring and evaluation. Identify timing and nature of review and conditions under which, and process whereby, policy change will be undertaken. Assign responsibilities for above.

Element 11: Measurable policy goals

Policy interventions are intended to achieve goals in relation to identified problems, and it would be expected that goals would be clearly expressed in policy statements, and form the reference point for implementation, monitoring and review. Yet in many cases goals are stated in vague terms and cause difficulties later in the cycle. For an adaptive approach, the stated goals are absolutely central to later evaluation, learning and improvement, and for that reason are separated here as a distinct element. Policy goals are different to social goals – sustainability is a social goal, whereas reduction targets for greenhouse gas emissions, or the defined degree of uptake of pollution-reducing technologies in an industry sector, are policy goals within that more general domain.

The term "measurable" is important. Policy goals stated in vague terms may be highly problematic when the policy intervention is evaluated, as there will be uncertainty as to the extent to which it has succeeded. In adaptive management, interventions in natural systems are ideally stated as hypotheses, to be applied, tested and learned from. Such strict statement of hypotheses is often difficult in complex policy situations characterised by multiple factors and uncertainty, but policy goals should nevertheless wherever practicable be stated in such a way as to allow later evaluation and public accountability. Central to measurability is the requirement that goals can be measured against a baseline representation of the current situation. Without such a baseline it will not be possible to assess performance. Stating measurable goals need not force unrealisable strictness and unrealistic expectations. Measurability may be achieved through definition of the *direction of change* as well as or instead of the *extent* of change, or through a range rather than a precise point or a minimum standard rather than a maximum or optimal state.

As well as the practical value of well-defined goals to enable and enhance evaluation, discussion of goals is necessary to promote a more inclusive and deliberative policy style, through the process of reaching agreement or at least understanding over the intent of a policy. Mutual understanding of goals reduces the probability of irreconcilable expectations being held by different policy actors, and furthermore will also reduce the chance of unexposed and unrealistic expectations on the part of some actors.

In defining goals, two key considerations apply. The first is the difference between goals that express desired outcomes in terms of *process* or *product*. While the intended result of most policy interventions is a product – a positive change in the environment, human society or natural–human system interactions – these products will arise from policy and management *processes*, and in some cases a new or improved process will be the principal outcome. The sorts of goals defined for either will be different and it is likely that the goals defined for a policy program will include both.

The second consideration is whether goals should be expressed in *quantitative* or *qualitative* terms. Quantitative goals are easier to measure progress against, and as long as the goals are well-formulated and meaningful may be less open to contest and disagreement. But in many situations quantitative goals may not be able to be expressed, either because of uncertainty or missing information or the nature of the intended outcome. Many people, particularly scientists, suspect qualitative goals and analysis. Properly stated, though, qualitative policy goals and targets may be just as useful as quantitative goals and are particularly relevant to process goals. In any case, a policy program would generally utilise both quantitative and qualitative goals. For anyone who questions the role and validity of qualitative principles and judgments, brief consideration of the role and power of legal doctrines or informal norms in society should convince them that this is not the case. As stressed in Chapter 2 and elsewhere in this book, policy decisions almost always involve political – that is, value-based and qualitative – judgments made on the basis of a range of information inputs only some of which will be quantitative.

Clearly, the number and kinds of goals that might be expressed in environment and sustainability policy is enormous, varying across issues, problems, policy instruments, social and political contexts, and time. To illustrate, Table 6.3 uses examples of process and product goals, both qualitative and quantitative, in a less measurable and thus problematic form, and in a more measurable form that is more suited to monitoring, evaluation and accountability.

These examples are specific and are suitable to what were classified as micro-problems in the previous chapter. Usually, a hierarchy of goals will be defined across macro–meso–micro-problems addressed in a policy, with more detail and specification

Table 6.3: Examples of measurable policy goals

	Less measurable	*More measurable*
Process goals	Context: participation in catchment planning	
More quantitative example	Draft catchment plan will be prepared and made available for public comment.	A draft catchment plan will be prepared within 12 months, forwarded to nominated stakeholders, advertised in local newspapers, made available in municipal libraries, and be open to public comment for 30 days.
More qualitative example	Catchment planning will be undertaken through a process which incorporates the views of relevant stakeholders.	An advisory panel will be established, comprising members representing urban residents, grazing and horticultural industries, environmental groups and scientists.
Product goals	Context: conservation reserves	
More quantitative example	The reserve system will be extended to incorporate at least 10% of original ecosystems.	The reserve system will include at least 10% of each original vegetation alliance as defined by the 1995 classification by (specify).
More qualitative example	Recreational facilities will be developed in conservation reserves.	At least three reserves in each administrative division will be accessible by normal passenger vehicles, and camping facilities and walking tracks will be developed in two per division.

possible lower in the hierarchy. Nevertheless, even at the macro-level, greater measurability should be pursued.

In practical terms, there is likely to be resistance to specifying goals (this is, separate to the difficulty of defining goals). The resistance may be *political* (reluctance to establish a provable basis for attributing blame for policy failure), or it may be *scientific* (reluctance to define desirable or sufficient states in the face of uncertainty). In some cases, such reluctance may be under-standable and justified. To address such situations, three strategies can be considered. First, a process of policy formulation that involves all relevant parties and respects their inputs and pers-pectives is more likely to allow the definition of common goals than a less inclusive process. Second, an adaptive approach would allow recognition of the difficulty or unclear scope of some goals and would both recommend a sequential set of goals and utilise cycles of implementation, monitoring and review over time. Third, for situations of deep uncertainty or contest, the institutionalisation of ongoing opportunities for discourse in the policy process may allow eventual clarification of agreed goals. In such situations, the tentative status of goals should be made explicit throughout the next stage of the policy cycle: implementation.

Chapter 7

POLICY IMPLEMENTATION

STAGE III: Policy implementation

Element 12:   Selecting policy instruments
Element 13:   Planning implementation
Element 14:   Planning communication
Element 15:   Assessing statutory, resource, etc requirements
Element 16:   Planning enforcement and compliance
Element 17:   Establishing monitoring provisions

This chapter summarises requirements for addressing elements 12–17 of the framework. The chapter covers a large number of elements, and some that are particularly important – especially policy instrument choice, where causes of policy failure are often located. Although we will continue to step through the elements of the implementation stage, the elements will not always be addressed in strict sequence, but will be attended to concurrently.

Element 12: Policy instrument choice

The choice of policy instrument and subsequent implementation are for many people the most visible and "sharp" parts of the policy process, and critical to achieving policy goals. A mechanical analogy emphasises the task – it may be apparent what part of an engine has to be fixed (element 8), and the end state that is desired (elements 9–11), but without the correct tool or set of tools little will be achieved. Governments and interacting non-government groups have an array of policy instruments available to them. However, not all instruments will be suitable in a given situation and how to choose the most appropriate instrument/s is not always clear. Indeed, it is often not clear how or why a particular instrument has been chosen.

Many policy texts refer to policy instruments as "implementation instruments", logically enough as instruments are used to implement a government's wishes and achieve stated objectives.

Here, however, "implementation" refers to both the third general stage in the policy process discussed in this chapter, and a specific element (13) that follows instrument selection.

Too often a limited range of instruments is considered. There may be good reason for deeming some options impractical, undesirable or irrelevant – for example, draconian regulation for a minor problem, or slow and gentle educational programs for large and urgent ones. However, it is necessary that early in consideration of instrument choice a full menu is acknowledged, and criteria for choice stated. The main purpose of this section is to present and explain such a menu and set of selection criteria. To bring us to that point, however, we can consider a characterisation of a limited process of instrument choice.

Debates about policy instruments commonly recognise just a few general categories, notably regulation, education, and market-based approaches, but also increasingly self-regulation and community-based programs. Just as commonly, the general superiority of one or other category is advocated over others by different policy actors, with the classic argument being between the merits of regulation versus market mechanisms. Some policy actors advocate one kind of instrument as suitable for many or even all problems. This puts the means before the ends and narrows the scope of policy options. This is, however, to be expected, remembering that political ideology or disciplinary leaning play a strong role in determining what policy options will be favoured.

There are three crucial problems with such simplistic debates. First, it is foolish to imagine that one kind of policy instrument will always or even usually be superior to others, given the diversity of problems and contexts in environment and sustainability. Sometimes one will be more useful, sometimes another. While crude, ideological advocacy of one instrument over another is unfortunate, such is the nature of politics and these contests will always occur, but we can perhaps frame them more productively. If we understand that the fundamental task is to change individual or collective behaviours so that some goal can be achieved, then we can understand policy instruments as "messages" that seek to drive that change. Policy instruments might convey the required message in a harsh manner, such as making a polluting activity liable to criminal conviction and thus imprisonment, or very large fines or other financial disincentives such as strong taxation measures. Or, the message may be gentle, such as a public aware-ness campaign or a modest financial incentive (for example, a tax deduction or grant) or disincentive (small fines or tax liabilities). Policy instrument choice in this sense is a more neutral matter – although never fully "objective" – of choosing the *best medium to deliver the message*. That message might be a plea, rational argu-ment, a price signal, moral exhortation, helpful information, or a threat.

Second, categories such as "regulatory" or "market-based" are general classes of instrument, not meaningful and precise descriptions or choices. There is a great diversity of specific options within each class (see Table 7.1 below). To advance an argument that regulation or market mechanisms or community-based approaches are "best" is not only unhelpful, but in fact meaningless. For example, different market mechanisms exist, and different forms of education or regulation, and each is quite different from another.

Third, it is rare that a policy intervention utilises only one instrument, even when a specific one represents a major feature. Recent recognition of the need for "mixed instrument" approaches in fact ignores that public policy has, in theory if not always in practice, recognised this for some time. Environment and sustaina-bility policies are interventions in interdependent human–natural systems, and complex tasks that demand complex interventions. Even the most simple and narrow problem will require a package of instruments, as a quick example will show. Product category X has been shown to be environmentally damaging, and there is sufficient consensus that consumption of it should be discouraged, with the debated options being a price signal via a tax on the product, to slowly discourage use, or a regulatory approach that removes the product from the market place more quickly. If a tax is chosen, this will require a legislative basis, an education program to explain it, and organisational capacity to administer it. If the regulatory path is followed, the legislative base, administrative capacity and education program will be required, as will a compensation package for affected producers. In the case of more complex problems such as landscape-scale biodiversity con-servation or salinity control, the complexity will be even greater. No policy instrument is an island.

In practice, policy analysts and officials may have little choice in selecting instruments, but simply have to respond to decisions

Table 7.1: Policy instruments for environment and sustainability

Instrument class	Main instruments and approaches (selected)
1. Research and development: monitoring of human-natural systems	Increase knowledge generally (basic research) or specifically (applied research), intended to: inform setting of a goal or standard; develop technologies or practices; establish socio-economic implications; or monitor environmental conditions, human development or policy impact.
2. Creating new or improving existing communication and information flows	*Directions*: research findings to policy; policy imperatives to research; both to firms, agencies and individuals. *Mechanisms*: sustainability indicators; state of the environment reporting; natural resource accounting; community-based monitoring; environmental auditing; mechanisms for consultation or policy debate.
3. Education and training	Public education (moral suasion); targeted education (sub-sets of population); formal education (schools, universities); training (skills development); education regarding other instruments.
4. Consultative	Mediation; negotiation; dispute resolution; inclusive institutions and processes.
5. Agreements and conventions	Intergovernmental agreements/policies (international or within federations); memoranda of understanding; conventions and treaties.
6. Statute law	New statutes or regulations under existing law to: create institutional arrangements; establish statutory objects and agency responsibilities; set aside land for particular uses; enable land use planning and development control; enforce standards; prohibit practices; create punitive measures.
7. Common law	Applications of doctrines such as negligence, nuisance, public trust.
8. Covenants on title	Pro-environment provisions tied to property title.
9. Assessment procedures	Review of effects; environmental impact assessment; social impact assessment; cumulative impact assessment; strategic environmental assessment; risk assessment; life cycle assessment; statutory monitoring requirements.
10. Self-regulation	Codes of practice, codes of ethics, professional standards within an industry or profession.

Instrument class	Main instruments and approaches (selected)
11. Community involvement	Participation in policy formulation; freedom of information laws; rights to comment on development proposals; community-based monitoring; community implementation of programs; cooperative management; community ownership and management.
12. Market mechanisms	Input or output taxes/charges; use charges; subsidies; rebates; penalties; tradable emission permits or use quotas; tradable property/resource rights; performance assurance bonds; deposit-refund systems.
13. Institutional or organisational change	New or revised settings, to enable other instruments or policy and management generally, especially over time.
14. Change other policies	Removal or reform of distorting subsidies, conflicting policies or statutory objects.
15. Inaction	Where justified by due consideration, and generally involving commitment to reconsider the issue at a later date.

already made. Such a choice may be the result of implicit analysis of alternatives, or it may be a non-analytical product of disciplinary bias or political ideology. The status and irreversibility of such a decision will vary: some instrument choices are backed by an easily reversed policy decision whereas others might be expressed in a less easily changed legislative package (for example, a tradable resource rights regime in a new fisheries or water management Act). Even in a case where the instrument has been predetermined, a comparative analysis of instruments and criteria for choice will sharpen understanding of the relative merits of the instrument and improve the prospects for effective implementation. The fact that one instrument will need to be supported by others in a mix also instructs us to consider multiple options even where a major part of the policy package is already determined.

Policy instruments and criteria for choice

Table 7.1 sets out a menu of policy instruments for environment and sustainability, organised under general instrument classes. While not dissimilar to menus found in general policy texts, it is more detailed than most, and styled specifically for the sustainability domain. Some classes and instruments that some people would view as very important are not identified explicitly. For example, product and building design are key determinants of environmental impact, as is urban planning, but in the menu in Table 7.1 these would be pursued by instruments such as regulatory standards, formal education, land use planning, and so on. The menu presented here attempts not to confuse ends (outcomes) with means (instrument types).[1]

This menu presents instrument choice as complex, but it does represent the richness of options available. Even after indicating the detail that lies beneath the general instrument classes, Table 7.1 is only a summary, and more detailed options and policy design possibilities exist for instruments presented in a singular sense. For example, there is a greater variety of participatory policy approaches than indicated above (see Chapter 9) and in strategic environmental assessment (SEA) many variations in targets and procedures are possible (see Chapter 10, and Marsden and Dovers 2002).

Selecting specific instrument types will be followed by detailed analysis and design of features of the instrument, however that finer resolution task is not covered further here.

Selection from a wide range of instruments may be impossible in some cases, especially where a government or powerful groups within a policy network pre-empt choice by prescribing an instrument class – for example a market mechanism or regulatory response – before any proper analysis is undertaken. At least, a detailed menu will make clear the more specific choices within classes, and selecting from that sub-menu provides an opportunity to consider the pros and cons of the choice made and of alternatives. To do that, the attributes of different instruments relative to the problem at hand can be explored through *criteria for instrument choice*.

How to choose the best option is no easy task but a set of criteria can provide guidance or at least can structure debate and analysis. Table 7.2 presents a set of criteria, divided into those determining the most effective instrument in a "perfect world" (that is, without implementation constraints), and those affecting

---

1   This categorisation of policy instruments differs somewhat from many in the policy literature (eg the characterisation by Hood (1986)). The main reason for the difference is that Table 7.1 seeks to reflect the range of policy instruments commonly proposed or used in the sustainability and environmental fields in some detail, rather than a more generic and less detailed list applicable to any situation. Many specific instruments (although fewer classes) in the Table are particular to sustainability and environment. See also Sterner 2002.

the practicalities of implementation. As with the instrument menu, some of these criteria are commonly found in general policy texts, some are particular to environment and sustainability.

This is not a definitive list and other criteria could be developed, but it captures the main considerations that should inform instrument choice. Taking the menu and criteria together the task is not made easier, but is made more informed. One criterion may be more or less important in a given situation than another, such as flexibility (1e) in the face of uncertainty, or dependability (1b) in the case of an urgent and serious problem. However, no single criterion, even dependability, will be the only consideration. They are to some extent related (for example, equity impacts and political feasibility), and will always be traded off against one another (for example, dependability versus cost). Importantly, as well as aiding choice or at least helping to structure analysis, consideration of a full set of criteria will assist later policy design by identifying possible weaknesses of an otherwise favoured instrument and thus allowing remedial strategies to be developed. For example, the criterion of institutional feasibility may be problematic, but that may not rule an instrument out but rather prompt institutional or organisational change.

The issue of flexibility (1e) in Table 7.2 raises a critical issue. In Chapter 5, uncertainty and the precautionary principle (PP) were discussed, and a core element of the precautionary principle – "serious and *irreversible*" – might be applied to policy instruments. Given uncertainty as to the effectiveness and impact of policy interventions (and thus instruments), a strong burden of proof might be expected to be placed on proposals for a policy change which is uncertain in its impact and also is irreversible. For example, the decision to privatise an important water resource management function (for example, residing a water agency) to realise efficiency gains at the risk of loss of environment al protection functions or participatory resource management opportunities, is for practical political purposes irreversible. To seek the same efficiency benefits via limited-term, competitive contracting-out of functions is a reversible strategy, and might be justified more easily in the face of uncertainty.

Some further comments on instrument choice are warranted. Despite arguing strongly above that no instrument or instrument class is better, there are *universal policy instruments* required to some degree in any policy package. These three are: a basis in

Table 7.2: Selection criteria for policy instruments

Criteria	Explanation
1. Effectiveness criteria:	Determining the likelihood of the instrument achieving goals in the absence of constraints.
(a) information requirements	Is the information required to design the instrument available within the required timeframe?
(b) dependability	Will the instrument be more likely than other options to achieve the outcomes required?
(c) corrective versus antidotal focus	Does the instrument target proximate or underlying factors; that is, address causes rather than symptoms?
(d) systemic potential	Related to 1c above, does the instrument have system-wide potential, influencing widespread causes of sustainability problems?
(e) flexibility in space and time	Can the rate or style of application of the instrument be varied depending on context, or as the situation or status of knowledge changes?
(f) efficiency (re dependability)	Will the instrument achieve the desired goals in an efficient manner – ie more unit of outcome per unit of investment?
(g) Complexity and cross-sectoral influence	Can the instrument be well-targeted, with either fewer or identifiable/controllable impacts on other policy or social goals?
2. Implementation criteria:	Determining the likelihood of the instrument being successfully advocated and implemented.
(a) equity implications	Who bears the costs of the application and impact of the instrument, and is this equitable or fair (includes the polluter-pays principle)?
(b) cost	Is the gross cost (especially financial, but also human, organisational and informational resources) bearable in a practical sense (nb: this is an additional consideration to what instrument is the most efficient)?

Criteria	Explanation
(c) social/political feasibility	Is the instrument likely to be deemed acceptable socially or politically by key groups or the public?
(d) institutional feasibility	Does adequate institutional/organisational capacity exist for design and implementation of the instrument?
(e) monitoring requirements	Can the uptake of the instrument and/or its impact or effectiveness be monitored?
(f) enforcement/avoidability	Can the intended impact (ie behaviour change) be avoided, and if so can the uptake or impact of the instrument be enforced (this applies not only to regulatory instruments)?
(g) communicability	Can the logic, nature and implications of the instrument be communicated to affected parties, upon who will depend the successful application of the instrument?

statutory (or possibly customary or common) law, in societies subject to the rule of law; an educative component, because people need to know what is going on for a policy to work; and institutional/organisational provisions, because it is only through institutions that common goals can be pursued.

The final consideration is to stress the importance of criteria 1c and 1d, and of utilising *systemic policy instruments* that address underlying causes rather than more superficial, "band-aid" policy approaches. If a sustainability problem is serious and has causal roots deep in human systems (Chapter 3), then instruments with systemic and corrective effect should be considered. For example, it may be that fossil energy use must be significantly reduced to reduce greenhouse gas emissions. Energy use is fundamental to modern societies and economies and is a systemic cause of greenhouse gas emissions (and other environmental problems). A well-designed carbon tax, increased in a predictable fashion over time and with appropriate investment of the proceeds to encourage alternatives, would be a systemic policy instrument, more so than, say, a myriad of smaller grants and educative programs. Other examples of systemic instruments, or systemic versions of instruments, include widespread curricula reform to influence the knowledge and skills of future generations (as opposed to superficial environmental education), or the firm statutory expression of sustainability principles with accompanying methodological guidance, thus instructing all public decision-makers to give sustainability higher priority (as opposed to vague, discretionary iterations of principles in the objects clause of legislation).

Matching these two criteria to the sorts of problems where they are most suited suggests a further step in instrument choice so as to best fit the "tool" to the task. This is jointly considering (a) the instrument menu, (b) the selection criteria, and (c) a framework identifying the specific attributes of environmental and sustainability policy problems (element 8, Chapter 5, and the discussion in Chapter 3). This allows the attributes of the policy instrument, reflected through the criteria, to be connected more with the attributes of the problem being confronted.

Some of the criteria in Table 7.2 indicate important considerations that will now be discussed as separate elements: implementation, communication, enforcement, and policy monitoring.

Element 13: Implementation plan

The plan of implementation of a policy may be incorporated sufficiently in the policy statement and associated discussion and documentation, and is inherent in other elements. However, it is sufficiently important to warrant identification as an element in its own right. Also, the pathway of implementation is rarely static; changes will occur and be responded to. For a start, once policy goals (element 11) and specific instruments (element 12) have been defined, the implementation task will change and become more detailed. Also, early experiences with implementing instruments, resourcing that implementation, and so on, will rarely proceed as initially envisaged. The implementation plan should be viewed as a dynamic process and document, not a one-off or static task. Nevertheless, at the stage following instrument choice, revisiting implementation is particularly important, and the essential elements of an implementation planning exercise at that stage will typically include the following:

- An analysis of the chosen instrument/s to ascertain and arrange for specific requirements for implementation, including:

- further information requirements for the key policy officials:
- information needs of others who will be involved and/or affected, and how this information can be generated and communicated (element 14);
- statutory, administrative and resource requirements for effectively implementing the instrument/s (element 15);
- issues of enforcement and compliance, including resourcing and responsibility (element 16);
- design and enactment of a process of monitoring the uptake and effect of the instrument, including defining routine data capture and responsibilities for that (element 17);

• Definition and communication of roles in instrument implementation and access to information regarding implementation (general elements of participation, transparency, description and communication, see Chapter 9).

• A procedure for reflecting on the success of implementation during early stages, including the assigning of responsibilities for this.

It should be noted that careful consideration of criteria for instrument selection (element 12 and Table 7.2) will have provided a solid basis for these tasks and developed a familiarity with the implementation challenges associated with particular instruments. This reinforces the value of utilising the selection criteria even when the instrument has been pre-determined. But given that the individuals involved in a policy exercise may change along the way and analysis from element 12 may not be available later, it is worth reiterating the process. That way the importance of later implementation and evaluation elements (14–19) will be reinforced.

Element 14: Communication and information plan

Element 13 (see above), the policy statement at element 10, and the general elements of public participation and communication, should set out the broad style and some specific elements of an information and communication strategy for the implementation stage. However, it is again advisable to revisit this element following instrument selection and design and implementation planning, as the particular forms of information and the specific audiences for communication can be defined at a finer resolution.

The specific information and communication needs will vary across instruments, jurisdictions and other variables, but key forms of information include:

- The detailed features of the specific instrument selected, including explanation of variable features and why a particular level or rate of application has been chosen. For example, in the case of a tax instrument, the rate or rates applied, exemptions, qualifying requirements, responsible authority, registration of application processes, appeal processes, and so on. Or for conservation grants, the amounts available, application processes, eligibility requirements, and so on.

- Descriptions of variation across the contexts where the instrument will be applied; for example, the size, resourcing and other features of the educational organisations through which a formal educational measure can be delivered, or the relative size and viability of potential markets in a catchment-based water trading system.

- The organisational capacities and human resource requirements for implementation (note, this is different and at a finer scale than element 15 below, which concerns institutional capacity within government). For example, the skill needs in a profession expected to implement a new code of practice, or the local organisational capacity for receiving and acquitting grants.

In terms of communicating necessary information about the policy package, instrument and its implementation, target audiences will vary. These differences are defined by the root purpose of all policy instruments – messages designed to prompt behaviour change. Thus, the audiences for communication are those individuals and groups for whom (a) the message is intended, and those (b) whose behaviour the message is meant to change. The two may not always be exactly the same, and across implementation contexts audiences may vary even for the same instrument. There will generally be multiple audiences with varying information needs, especially as most policy interventions involve multiple instruments. Given all this, and the quantity of different instrument options, a full description of possibilities here would be impossible and unwieldy so illustrative examples must suffice (Table 7.3).

Table 7.3: Information types and audience definition for implementation of different policy instruments (examples)

Instrument	Information types (simplified, illustrative examples)	Main audiences
Regulatory standard specifying outflow water quality for industry sector	Technical details of standards	Firms, operators, water agency staff
	Compliance regime (licensing process, inspection regime	All of the above, but also other possible enforcement agencies
	Sanctions (fines, licence suspensions)	All of the above, plus lawyers and courts
Local government rate rebate for biodiversity conservation on farms	Policy intent and rate structure	All residents, state or provincial government
	Application details	Eligible farmers
	Register of rebates, financial details (confidential)	Council auditors, State valuer-general, tax department
	Overall rebate cost and impact	All residents, State government, other interested councils
Carbon tax levied at "well-head" on fossil fuels, with revenue invested to fund renewables and energy efficiency	Intent and structure of policy	Industry, consumers, relevant departments
	Tax rates, details of payment schedule	Firms, tax officials, accounting industry
Statutory expression of sustainability principles in enabling legislation of non-environmental government agency	Intent of policy, detailed content of principles, roles and responsibilities, etc	Legislative drafters, affected portfolios, policy community, public
	Methods for implementation (eg risk assessment for precautionary principle)	Responsible authorities, agency staff, policy network, legal industry
	Appeals processes against decisions deemed inconsistent with principles	General public, policy community, staff, legal system and industry

Table 7.3 indicates that multiple tasks must be integrated within a communication strategy to engage different audiences. Even for the same type of information, communication strategies will differ according to the audience. The technical detail of a water quality standard, for instance, would be differently communicated to chemically trained operators and specialists than to a lay audience.

Importantly, audiences for communication activities should not be thought of as simply passive recipients of "received wisdom" from government or the inner circles of policy networks (see further Chapter 9). While such one-way information flow may at times be appropriate, in many cases it will not be. Many instruments require implementation by actors distant from the policy process (for example, trading in markets, participating in on-ground management, applying risk reduction procedures in workplaces). At least *two-way flows of information* between policy agencies and the public will feature, both in the implementation of the same instrument across varying contexts, and in monitoring and evaluation of the instrument's performance. This is a case where thoughtful consideration and ongoing implementation of context-specific applications of the general element of public participation is relevant.

Element 15: Statutory, institutional and resource requirements

This element forces attention on the capacity of the policy agency and others to properly implement the chosen policy instrument and undertake associated tasks. To revert to a mechanical analogy again, the problem with the broken-down engine has been identified, the desired state defined, and the repair task and requisite tools identified. But none of this is very useful in the absence of a workshop, permit to use some of the tools, and qualified and competent personnel. Key requirements to be considered and provided at this stage include legal basis, institutional settings and financial, human and information resources:

- *Legal competence and defensibility.* Public policies must be legally defensible – that is, not liable to challenge over their validity in the courts. Therefore, the legal basis for a new policy should be ensured, typically in statute law but also common law, and in some cases customary law. Moreover, the role of the law in non-regulatory areas is crucial and too often overlooked, such as defining agency objectives, guaranteeing public access to information, creating new organisational forms, and so on. Such roles will usually be provided through statutory law, whether regulations under existing legislation or new or amended legislation. Particularly with new or novel policy instruments or organisational strategies, the adequacy of the statutory setting requires close attention.

- *Institutional and organisational capacity.* Especially with novel or unfamiliar policy instruments, or traditional instruments being applied in new or untried sectors of the society or economy, care needs to be taken to ensure that there is the capacity to deliver. This can be divided into two aspects:

  - within the government agency or organisation with primary responsibility for policy implementation, for example the tax department, environmental protection authority or parks service; and
  - within agencies, organisations or non-government groups who will have delegated or subsidiary roles in implementation including information generation or dissemination, adjustment of other policies or monitoring.

- *Financial resources.* The most commonly recognised cause of policy failure is inadequate funding, even where the other requirements may be just as or even more important. This may be due to budget constraints under which governments operate, or to limits upon the amount of investment that private or community groups or individuals can make. If the level of funding for optimal implementation is unavailable – as will most likely be the case – it is nonetheless important to develop a realistic understanding of limits that available funding create relative to the scale of the problem and especially possibly unrealistic expectations in the policy community. Over-optimistic expectations make policy failure certain, whereas realistic understanding of the limits of the policy invites consideration of supplementary or additional policy initiatives. In other cases poor analysis or prediction of the costs of policy implementation may be the problem and, although this may be unavoidable, the better the analysis and planning of funding, the less chance of unforeseen deficiencies.

- *Human resources.* Often, the need for new or extended human resources or knowledge and skills on the part of agency staff is an overlooked requirement that appears as crucial only in retrospect.[2] Two broad aspects of this exist: the *quantity* of human resources (for example, number of staff); and the *quality* of human resources (knowledge, skills, preparedness). While the quantity issue seems obvious it is a constant issue, especially in the environment and sustainability domain where the number and complexity of tasks is increasing and often the number of staff has decreased through public sector reform. The quantity of human resources can be attended through adjustments to numbers of people, or through adjustments to individual and group workloads. Human resources may be "in-house" or regular staff, continuing or temporary, or externally provided in the form of consultants. The realities of long-term and adaptive policy approaches warn against only allowing for staff resources in the short term. This applies especially to the use of consultants and short-term staff in agencies because of down-sizing over time, and where these temporary additions to human resources may be performing functions of longer-term relevance, with the result that institutional memory and skills become fragmented.

    On quality we can recognise three broad areas of skills and capacities:

    - background knowledge regarding the logic of the policy approach chosen, especially if the instrument is unfamiliar or substantially different from previous

---

2   For a more detailed discussion of two cases where human capacity proved important in the New Zealand context, see Connor and Dovers (2004). A critical weakness of the landmark Resource Management Act was the insufficient support given to and human capacity developed in local (district) councils to support implementation of a complex new policy regime. In contrast, the introduction of the New Zealand fisheries Quota Management System – an internationally remarkable example of a property rights regime – the issue of understanding and skills development within government and in the industry community was better addressed and was crucial to successfully embedding a radically different policy approach.

routine experience (for example, community-based approaches being applied by an agency with a history of regulatory measures, or a market instrument by a planning agency);
- technical knowledge and skills concerning the instrument in question;
- contextual knowledge of the sectors, regions, community sub-groups or industries where the instrument will be implemented.

Outside the primary agency, this issue is also crucial, but has been covered at element 14 above. However, in the case of complex partnerships in policy design and implementation, which are becoming increasingly common, the division between government as creators and community as recipients of policy does and should break down, and considerations such as human resources in non-government (especially community-based) groups become more important.

- (*Information resources* are also relevant, especially in association with human resources; see element 14 above).

Mostly, all these requirements will be attended to within the primary agency, but also other agencies in the increasingly common case of inter-agency or whole-of-government policy implementation, and in the wider policy community.

An aid to considering these requirements is to identify the attributes of institutions and organisations, as a checklist of institutional capacities, to be analysed against the nature of the problem and the tasks it presents. Table 7.4 presents one version of such attributes, serving both as an analytical technique and as a reminder of the complex nature of institutional settings. The attributes in Table 7.4 are both generic and neutral: other versions can be specific to a policy sector such as sustainability (see Chapter 10), or framed as "positive" institutional attributes that are believed to favour sustainability.[3]

---

3   Table 7.4 is taken from Dovers and Mobbs (1997); for more general discussions and definition of attributes, see North (1990), Ostrom (1990) and Goodin (1996).

Table 7.4: Checklist: institutional attributes versus problem set

Institutional attributes (of existing or proposed institutional and organisational setting for policy implementation)	Relevance to and match with problem set
Extent or limits in geographical space (spatial scale)	(eg) OK
Jurisdictional, political and administrative boundaries	(eg) needs reform
Degree of permanence and longevity	(eg) n/a
Intended or actual roles (informational, cultural, legal, economic, etc)	etc
Sectoral or issue coverage/focus	etc
Nature and source of aims and mandate (in custom, policy statement, or statute or common law)	
Degree of independence/autonomy	
Accountability (how, to whom)	
Formality or informality of operation	
Political nature and support (actual, required)	
Exclusiveness/inclusiveness (membership, representativeness)	
Degree of community awareness and acceptance (actual, required)	
Degree of functional and organisational flexibility across time and contexts	
Resourcing requirements (financial, human, material)	
Information requirements (internally and externally driven or met)	
Existence of or need for linkages with other parts of the institutional system	

Element 16: Enforcement and compliance

Part of implementation of any instrument is the uptake of that instrument. In policy circles, the terms "enforcement" and "compliance" are generally associated with direct regulatory ("command-and-control") instruments, however while compliance is particularly relevant to regulatory strategies the terms and what they entail should be applied to a range of instruments. If a regulation is avoided or breached, a tax measure evaded, a positive financial incentive not utilised, an industry code of practice ignored or unnoticed, or a public education message unheard, then implementation has to some extent failed. The degree of failure is closely related to the proportion of the target population disregarding, evading or unaware of the instrument. Perfect compliance or uptake is virtually impossible, and introducing the notion of compliance early in the policy process should prompt some consideration of what degree of compliance would be acceptable compared to policy goals. This would result in a refinement of policy goals and a better understanding of monitoring requirements (elements 17–19).

This element reminds policy networks and authorities to consider compliance and possible enforcement measures during the implementation design stage, rather than retrofit these aspects later when problems arise. Apart from better policy design and a more proactive and effective policy process, this will result in a better understanding of resourcing and communication requirements, and of ongoing monitoring needs. We can identify four kinds of compliance relevant to various policy instruments:

- *Compliance in undertaking assigned responsibilities* for implementation on the part of responsible authorities and others involved in implementation such as government staff. Such responsibilities could include field inspections, record-keeping, information dissemination, evaluation, and so on.

- *Compliance by those directly affected* by the instrument, or who are targets of the instrument, outside of responsible agencies, such as firms, individuals or households in the case of regulatory instruments, industry associations who are required to provide data, or educational authorities required to undertake curriculum change.

- *Compliance with enabling or subsidiary aspects*, within and outside of government, aside from the primary agency or groups. For example, subsidiary activities may be required of other agencies in implementation, such as where a statistical agency is responsible for collecting data relating to some aspect of the policy intervention. This is especially relevant where more than one agency or level of government is involved, such as the example in Table 7.3 of local rate rebates where a state/provincial or national government body plays a minor but important role as registrar.

- *Uptake of voluntary measures.* While "compliance" is a strong word for such uptake, including this category does emphasise that voluntary uptake can be just as important to policy success as more forced obedience.

Enforcement is required in two circumstances: (a) where it is believed that regular inspection or data gathering and thus checking of performance will be necessary; and (b) when communication and persuasion to comply have failed and stronger measures will be required. Many enforcement strategies exist, to be chosen to match the form of compliance and the specific context, and range from gentle reminders through to threats of harsh penalties or public exposure. It is not necessarily only government and other official organisations that enforce policy; compliance and uptake can be pursued through a range of strategies including warnings from agencies, recourse to the courts, legal standing for community objectors, public monitoring and accountability, self-regulation in industry, or public shaming of firms or individuals.

To complete discussion of this element, we can return to the strong link between regulatory instruments and compliance and enforcement.[4] It is common now to hear the statement that "regulation doesn't work". Direct regulation was a mainstay policy response for many years, and in many cases did not succeed in reversing environmental degradation. However, it is often unclear whether a regulatory approach was inappropriate, the regulation was poorly designed, or it was poorly implemented and enforced. Enforcement is expensive, but so is proper implementation to ensure uptake of other instruments. Actual implementation of regulations is often different from the original intention or the "black letter law" version of what happens, and relatively little work on regulatory implementation (law-in-context research) has been carried out in the environmental area. The intentionally disparaging description of regulation as "command-and-control" policy, linking environmental regulation to repressive centrally planned societies, might often be better called "command-then-compromise" in reality.

---

4   For a fuller discussion of new approaches to regulation, see Gunningham and Grabosky (1999).

Empirically-based argument should be separated from ideological or theoretical advocacy, while accepting both as valid inputs to policy discussion (see Chapter 2). Opponents of regulation see an unwieldy administrative rationality and a wrongful belief that people only respond to imposed rules. These opponents include "woolly social scientists" who hold a communicative rationality that instructs cooperative and educational instruments, and "hard-nosed economists" who champion price signals in a free market as the prime way to influence rational, utility-maximising individuals. The position taken in this book is that these positions are all both partially true and singly inadequate, as all instruments are available as media for the message. A stiff price mechanism (for example, a prohibitive tax) or jolting public education campaign (for example, targeting car accidents or AIDS) may be no less strong messages than strict regulation. And all will take effort to implement and enforce.

Element 17: Policy monitoring provisions

This element instructs that policy monitoring provisions should be incorporated into the policy process as early as possible, not added as an afterthought and then forgotten. The next chapter deals with the detail of policy evaluation: here the intent is to discuss the basics of embedding the necessary functions so that later evaluation can be informed and effective.

Often a summary policy statement (element 10) will contain a provision stating that the policy will be reviewed, typically in a form such as "this policy will be reviewed in three years time". Although more detail or intention in terms of the nature of the review and evaluation may exist within an agency or in supplementary documentation, or indeed in key officials' heads, this is inaccessible and inconsistent with increasingly inclusive policy styles. If we understand policies as purposeful experiments in the face of uncertainty, complexity and a lack of proven, widely accepted approaches, then monitoring and evaluation of these experiments is crucial to learning and to improving capacities.

An all too common occurrence is for the vague promise of review to be forgotten; the need to review the policy then becomes apparent only when failure becomes obvious. In the meantime, responsibilities for monitoring the progress of the policy have not been assigned, or the matter is put aside as other issues emerge and the time and resources of the agency and associated groups in the policy community become diverted. The data necessary to assess policy performance have not been kept, and so the reasons for either policy success or failure cannot be learned. Thus policy ad hocery and amnesia occur.

To guard against this, we can propose a set of basic components of incorporation of policy monitoring at the implementation stage (prior warning of this need will occur when the criterion of monitoring requirements is considered during instrument selection):

- Recognise and cater for the inevitable link between *environmental monitoring* (elements 3–4) and monitoring of the impact of the policy instrument. In the absence of either, proper analysis of cause-and-effect will be difficult, as environmental change may swamp the impact of the policy intervention, or vice versa. Monitoring of the impact of other policies on the policy target may also be necessary, for example of the impact on financial pressures such as interest rates or cost-price trends on uptake of an environmentally sound technology being promoted through tax breaks and training schemes. This may require additional monitoring, or it may be achieved through linkage to existing monitoring and information streams.

- *Policy monitoring should closely relate to policy goals*, or rather to a measurable surrogate of policy goals that reflects the instruments used. For example, the policy goal of halting native vegetation clearance in a particular place can be measured against environmental monitoring, but the policy instruments used to encourage landholders not to clear – say, management training and biodiversity credit payments – are a separate matter to monitor.

- *Routine data capture* should be defined, so that necessary information is gathered along the way in readiness for review and evaluation, noting that such data may be difficult or impossible to obtain after the event.

- *Ongoing responsibilities* for data capture, storage and dissemination should be assigned from the start, whether in-agency, by consultants or by private firms or community groups.

- *A timetable for review and evaluation* of the policy should be developed, again with clear identification of responsibilities for both undertaking the review and acting upon its findings. Given the chance of unexpected developments in either natural or human systems, provision for flexibility in this and other components will be necessary.

As with other elements of the policy process, a complete approach to policy monitoring is likely to be impossible even if it was affordable. But as with other elements, getting closer to the ideal is better than being further away, and consideration of policy monitoring will provide a portrait of an ideal system against which the limits of what is done can be appreciated.

Chapter 8

POLICY MONITORING AND EVALUATION

STAGE IV: Policy monitoring and evaluation

Element 18:   Ongoing policy monitoring
Element 19:   Evaluating and reviewing processes
Element 20:   Extending, adjusting or ceasing policy

This chapter completes the discussion of the four stages of the policy cycle. It deals with the monitoring and evaluation of policies, viewing policies as uncertain interventions of an experimental nature in complex, interdependent natural and human systems. Although a summary, the importance of what comes after formulating and implementing a policy is emphasised. Indeed, it is better to regard monitoring and evaluation as an integral extension of policy implementation – a routine and central function – rather than as an afterthought or add-on to the "main game" of policy-making. The chapter deals with: monitoring in a general sense; data requirements; review and evaluation as a distinct phase; and communication and learning from evaluation. The particular demands of environment and sustainability are addressed along the way, as are feedbacks to other stages in the policy cycle.[1]

As with the entire cycle and framework, it is likely that it will not in practice be possible to address completely all that is described in this chapter. In such cases, it is nonetheless critical to embed in the policy process and community a sense of what full monitoring and evaluation would entail. This ensures that missing information and residual uncertainties are recognised and can be taken into account at a later point. We may never be able to do things perfectly, but recognition of incompleteness and imperfection is a prerequisite for learning, and a vast improvement on concealment or ignorance.

---

[1]   The arguments presented here are discussed in further detail in Dovers (2001), and the general topic of monitoring and information systems is covered in Venning and Higgins (2001).

Elements 18-19: Monitoring sustainability policy

An adaptive approach to environment and sustainability policy demands highly developed systems to gain, distribute and use information that describes the nature of the environment and human interactions with it. Ongoing monitoring (Chapter 5) forms the basis of this information resource, but core to human interventions in the environment, and in human production and consumption systems, are the policy interventions we mount to improve sustainability. This chapter deals with the monitoring of those interventions.

Monitoring and evaluation will inform adjustment of specific policy programs and instruments – that is the point of standard program evaluation in public policy and administration (see below). However, in the case of sustainability it is also likely to inform the reframing of problems (element 8), recognition of indirect causes of environmental degradation (elements 4–5), design of environmental monitoring systems (element 3), recognition of uncertainty (element 6), and feed into broader social debate about sustainability (element 1). It will also inform participatory design of policy processes (Chapter 9) and our evolving understanding of required organisational and institutional settings (Chapter 10). Constant reference between policy monitoring and ongoing tracking of human and natural systems is required. This is because policy interventions aim to alter the trajectory of parts of the linked human–natural system and the impacts of these interventions need to be identified amidst many other influences on system behaviour, including natural changes and those driven by other policies.

As noted in the previous chapter, provision for policy monitoring should be made in the implementation stage, with reference to policy goals, direct and indirect causes, and basic environmental monitoring. This is not irrelevant in other policy domains but is especially important in sustainability. The long-time scales of sustainability problems demand persistent monitoring, as policy interventions need to be maintained over considerable time before clear effects are evident in environmental conditions. Complexity in cause and effect within and across human and natural systems demands a sophistication in policy monitoring that combines targeted tracking of the policy intervention and connection with other systems of both policy and environmental monitoring. The need to integrate environmental, social and economic considerations makes policy monitoring an even more complicated task, as does the common requirement to meld quantitative and qualitative data and methods – it is often not possible to precisely or mathematically measure policy impact. Also, the involvement of multiple policy actors and interests means that multiple goals and outcomes will need to be accounted for.

Table 8.1 uses a simple example of a policy program aimed at sustainable agricultural land management and addressing four interrelated issues and problems. The example illustrates the complexity of tracking the impact of a policy intervention to account for biophysical variables, the main drivers of behavioural change and multiple interests and outcomes.

The example in Table 8.1 is simplified but realistic enough as a policy program and as an illustration of multiple interests and thus monitoring tasks, and of the connection between policy and environmental monitoring. A complication is the influence of indirect causes that may slow or halt the effect of a policy intervention but not be immediately apparent as a target for monitoring. In the case in Table 8.1, increased uptake of conservation tillage practices may after a time slow or cease. The reasons for this may not be obvious and could include saturation of the population of early adopters or emerging doubts in the farming community of the cost effectiveness of investing in changed tillage practices. On the other hand, it may be that another factor is operating, such as a rise in interest rates that negates the incentive of the tax rebate.[2]

This example indicates that policy monitoring is unlikely to be a discrete and tightly contained activity (although in some cases it may be), and that second and subsequent phases of monitoring and analysis are likely to be required as circumstances and knowledge change. That reflects the particular complexity and uncertainty associated with environment and sustainability problems, as well as the standard insight of traditional public policy, reflected in the policy cycle model, that policy is an iterative process.

---

[2]   This example draws on policy experiences in parts of the developed world during the high interest rate period of the late 1980s.

Table 8.1: Monitoring a policy intervention: Changing agricultural management practices

Substantive issue	Policy problem	Policy instrument	Key interests & outcomes	Monitoring implications
Soil erosion from crop lands	Increased use of conservation tillage methods	Education and technical advice; subsidised farm planning; tax rebates for new equipment	*Farmers:* maintain or improve profitability; costs of changing practices. *Govt:* maintain agricultural output	*Short term:* uptake of assistance packages; extent of conservation tillage. *Long term:* soil condition; stream sedimentation; agricultural productivity
Dryland salinity	Revegetate upper slopes	Grants and technical assistance for replanting	*Farmers:* prevent production losses. *Others:* downstream impacts on rivers	*Short term:* extent and survival of replanting. *Long term:* extent of salinised land; downstream salt loads
Biodiversity decline	Enhance habitat through revegetation of upper slopes and riparian land	Grants to community-based land care groups	*Environment groups:* wildlife protection and habitat connectivity over whole region. *Farmers:* on-farm wildlife	*Short term:* extent and survival of replanting. *Long term:* abundance of key species relative to baseline surveys
Downstream water quality	As above	As above	*Urban residents downstream:* urban water quality; costs of water treatment	Drinking water within stated quality standards for salts, sediments and nutrients; extent of treatment
All of the above	All of the above	All of the above	*Govt agency:* all of the above, plus accountability of expenditure	Acquittal of grant moneys; validity of tax rebate claims

Elements 18-19: Data requirements: Environmental and policy monitoring

The example given above indicates the numerous possible targets for policy monitoring and thus the sort of data that might need to be gathered. This will vary with the problem context and the policy approaches and instruments used, but data would be relevant to one of three categories:

- *Policy impact, effect or uptake,* measuring the extent to which the means used to effect behavioural or environmental change is being applied or used. Examples include the rate of uptake of a technology or practice, use of a tax rebate, awareness in a population of a communication package, frequency and volume of trade of a resource right, compliance with and prosecutions under a regulation, or access to and acquittal of community grants. This is the domain of standard approaches to policy evaluation.

- *Environmental and/or human conditions,* being the ends which are sought through the policy intervention. Examples include specific air or water quality parameters, emissions of pollutants, frequency and abundance of wildlife, or stock condition of a renewable resource. This is the domain of basic monitoring (element 3), but which in the case of sustainability is highly connected to policy monitoring.

- *Secondary influences,* both policy and environmental, which may be affecting the ability of the means to achieve the ends. Such factors include natural environmental variables (drought, wildlife species fluctuations, and so on) and policy variables (perverse incentives, countervailing communications).

Recognition of ends and means in this sense is a useful framing device for designing monitoring systems, and even though inherent in the policy cycle and framework, deserves emphasis. It demands the policy community and network state clearly: (a) what end and goals are being pursued and how progress can be tracked; (b) what means are being used to achieve this progress and how the success of these means can be measured in the interim; and (c) what other factors might influence achievement of the ends and how that influence can be identified.

The basis of policy monitoring is *routine data capture*. This refers to clearly identified data sets that are regularly gathered and maintained and are the responsibility of a particular individual, agency or group. Data necessary to eventual evaluation is often difficult to collect after the fact. When data gathering is left until the mandated review this will frustrate auditors and evaluators but more importantly will damage the prospects for rigorous analysis of success/failure and for learning and improvement.

Some flexibility in defining data requirements is necessary, but should ideally err on the side of conservatism and caution. That is, the ability must exist to capture new data streams should the need arise, but the discontinuation of a routine data collection must be carefully justified. Flexibility should not be an excuse to abandon data collection programs because of inattention or budget constraints. This flexibility indicates the way in which monitoring and evaluation can feed into discussion of desirable institutional settings. Often data will be gathered by actors operating in different agencies and problems with coordination will be exposed by difficulties in constructing monitoring systems, indicating the need for organisational change.

Crucial to monitoring is the assignment of responsibility for data gathering, storage and analysis. Rarely will monitoring be the responsibility of one actor or agency. For some straightforward aspects a designated part of an agency will have primary responsibility for tracking expenditures, grant applications, delivery of education kits, and so on. In most cases, however, multiple responsibilities will be assigned for multiple data streams. Using the example in Table 8.1, government officials from more than one agency, individual landholders, community-based environment groups and commissioned scientists could all conceivably be involved in ongoing monitoring activities. This requires not only clarity in assigning responsibilities, but also in communication and coordination across these different actors in accordance with the general elements explored in the next two chapters.

Although monitoring will generally be a shared responsibility amongst government and non-government players, there is a clear requirement for a central coordination and communication capacity to manage and disseminate information in a transparent fashion, and to provide long-term maintenance of databases. This will typically be a government role, although more inclusive bodies may undertake such a coordination function better if properly resourced and mandated to do so. The ability to store, transfer and make available data to multiple parties in multiple forms has increased significantly in recent times following developments in information and communication technologies (assuming sufficient technological capacity by all stakeholders). As well as multiple interests, it is likely that with any significant sustainability problem more than one jurisdiction will be involved, whether at national or sub-national level, and thus issues of data standardisation and ownership will need to be addressed.

Given the long time it may take for changes to be detectable in the environment, or for behavioural change to manifest in a society, often it will be the case that policy monitoring and environmental monitoring will concentrate less on "did it work?" and more on "are things heading in the right direction?" Getting useful messages from monitoring as time passes requires access to data in both raw and manipulated forms, and the maintenance of time series in databases. Over time, protocols and methods of data gathering and transformation will change, but a certain wariness of changing data standards too quickly is warranted, to protect the existence of longer time series of data. For many environmental trends, better a somewhat dated but maintained long-time series than two differently measured and incompatible data sets even where the later one is state-of-the-art.

With policy monitoring, as with basic environmental monitoring, a range of users of information will have not only varying interests but also quite different demands with respect to the level of detail. Senior policy-makers will rely on summary data or indicators and on the advice of others who are familiar with the detail, while researchers would have a greater interest in raw or detailed data than would many lay stakeholders. Often, a hierarchy of information is evident, moving from raw data, through manipulated and summary data, to broad indicators.

In environment and sustainability, there are now many systems of summary reporting for a wider audience in the form of state of environment (SoE) or sustainability reports. These are both generated from and aimed at the public, private and community sectors, at a range of scales from local through national to global. These typically avoid primary data in favour of reporting summary trends and composite indicators, and the extent to which such reports attend to policy monitoring varies. The conceptual and organising model most commonly used is that of pressure–state–response, which is used to organise information into: (a) human pressures on the environment; (b) the state of the environment and the effect those pressures have; and (c) responses society makes to address these (that is, policy interventions). Generally, SoE reports deal with "pressure" and "state" better and in more detail than "response" because rigorous and coordinated policy monitoring is not as common as it might be and policy monitoring is less amenable to straightforward quantitative measurement. It is doubtful, at least in the nearer term, whether such reporting can adequately capture policy monitoring and evaluation across a range of environment and sustainability problems and that this will best be attended to through evaluation of specific programs and of types of policy interventions.

Element 20: Review and evaluation, and policy change

This element entails a mandated review of a policy or program, the timing of which is set during the policy formulation and implementation stages (elements 10 and 17). From the perspective of adaptability, a set review may appear inflexible; however, the importance of assigning responsibility to work towards an informed evaluation is an essential discipline that will increase the chances that the policy will be evaluated. The actual timing of a review will vary according to the nature of the policy problems and instruments used, determined by the time it will conceivably take for a discernible impact to emerge, or for a useful quantity and quality of information to be generated. Depending on the context, a single review may be appropriate, or a mid-program review as well as a major review.

Also highly variable will be who undertakes a policy evaluation, and who is involved in the process of evaluation. Policy evaluations are most often undertaken either by government agency staff (many large agencies have dedicated evaluation staff), by an independent arm of government (for example, an auditor-general), or by commissioned consultants, who will engage with the policy community through surveys or consultations. Also, independent thinks tanks, NGOs and researchers may undertake policy evaluations, as may committees of parliaments, or special commissions of inquiry. In the case of sustainability, the extended policy community and participatory nature of programs means that such inclusion of stakeholders in evaluation is especially important. This may be achieved through consultation, focused meetings, submissions and so on, or by inclusion of stakeholder representatives as part of the evaluation team.

This points to two broad purposes of evaluation. The first is evaluation aimed largely at ensuring efficiency and accountability in expending government program funds, of interest to stake-holders but typically the responsibility of those within the relevant policy network. The second is evaluation aimed at assessing the impact of the policy in addressing sustainability, and the lessons that can be learned from the experience, of interest to the wider policy community. These two suggest somewhat different modes of undertaking evaluations, and although it is possible to address both at the same time the different purposes should be recognised.

The first purpose is an important function and responsibility in a public administration context where governments need to ensure accountability and effectiveness in expending public resources and the effectiveness of their own efforts. Standard program evaluation is covered in many evaluation procedures and summarised in most general policy texts, and for this reason the following simply notes major forms.[3] This form of evaluation is what Howlett and Ramesh (2003) term administrative evaluation, aimed at ensuring that policies produce results at the least possible cost, and within which they define five strands that suggest different rationalities, approaches and data needs:

- *effort evaluation* driven by efficiency concerns, examining the quantity of inputs (time, finance, and so on) that have been used;

- *performance evaluation,* examining the outputs and outcomes of a policy in whatever form these have manifested (independent of whether the policy goals are being achieved);

- *adequacy of performance (effectiveness) evaluation,* which concentrates on whether the stated policy goals are being achieved;

- *efficiency evaluation,* exploring whether the outcomes of a policy program could have been achieved at a lower cost; and

---

[3] For example, Chapter 9 in Howlett and Ramesh (2003); Leeuw et al (1999); Patton (1997); and see the journal *Evaluation.*

- *process evaluation*, which seeks lessons about process and organisational design from individual programs.

In practice, a review and evaluation process will attend more than one of these, utilising different approaches, involving different policy actors, and requiring different forms of information.

Administrative evaluation has the same limits as the traditional rational–comprehensive model of policy-making discussed in Chapter 3. The logic of straightforward evaluation assumes a reasonably discrete, linear process, relatively few measurable variables, and an "end point" to the policy process relative to the policy problem. It is increasingly recognised, in all policy domains, that these assumptions are rarely met in the real world of complex problems. As argued in Chapter 3, this is especially the case with sustainability and more significant environmental problems, where long-term human and natural processes, pervasive uncertainty, complexity and multiple values render the rational-comprehensive model especially problematic.

Therefore it is necessary to not rely only on administrative evaluation, but to broaden the scope of evaluation over time, over multiple interests in a more participatory manner, and targeting long-term policy learning more than only near-term program efficiency and outcomes. It is not an either/or situation, but one where shorter term, linear program evaluation of individual policy programs is necessary in and of itself, but also as a feedstock of lessons feeding into longer term, composite learning processes across specific policies, sectors and time. This leads to two important considerations: what we seek to learn from multiple policy experiments, discussed in the next section; and the institutional settings that can allow such learning (Chapter 10).

Policy or problem change: Adaptation and learning

Evaluation should inform future policy action regarding, broadly, whether to: (a) discontinue the policy as the problem has been satisfactorily resolved; (b) persevere with much the same policy because it appears to be working although the problem remains and goals have not yet been achieved; (c) substantially redesign the policy to address failure to achieve the goals; or (d) redefine the policy problem in the light of experiences to date. All these involve *policy learning,* a crucially important concept introduced in Chapter 2 and, except for (a) above, they indicate a deliberate return to a previous stage of the policy cycle. Perseverance with much the same policy (b) indicates a return to Stage III of the policy cycle; redesign of the policy to Stage II, and reframing of the problem to Stage I. In situations of multi-part problems and complexity, the reality is often a return to more than one stage and element for different parts of the problem set. While a particular policy program will often be ceased or altered to the extent that it is essentially a wholly new program,[4] in the case of sustainability it will be rare that sustainability problems will have been made to "go away" and what in fact occurs is that we learn more about a problem and then address it in different and hopefully more effective ways.

Policy learning may take different forms (Table 8.2), all of which are essential under different circumstances, and are often pursued concurrently both in evaluation and in the monitoring that leads up to that. Of course, this indicates a continuing theme – that a range of policy actors and interests be involved in monitoring, evaluation and the subsequent lessons learned. The following expands on the summary of policy learning in Chapter 2.

Across contexts, the nature of policy learning will vary and the categories in Table 8.2 are useful as a device to think about how to maximise learning opportunities in a manner that recognises and accommodates different needs. Instrumental and government learning address how better to pursue *existing goals* within the prevailing construction of social and policy problems. Social and political learning, on the other hand, allow for and in fact deliberately seek learning about new ways to frame social goals and policy problems. Environment and sustainability problems demand attention to be paid to both.

Recalling previous discussions, different forms of learning invite the use of various approaches to monitoring and evaluation, as well as the involvement of different actors. Within government agencies, the dominant purpose of evaluation will be instrumental and government learning. However, in the face of uncertainty and

---

[4]   Often, what is promoted as a "new" policy launched by a government will in fact be largely the continuation of the policy program of a previous administration or even one of their own. Such rebadging is a political reality that makes more difficult but does not remove the need for continuity in policy monitoring and learning.

Table 8.2: Policy learning: forms and purposes

Form	What is learned?	Who learns?	To what effect?
Instrumental learning	How well instruments have allowed the achievement of goals.	Members of the policy network, especially government officials engaged in policy formulation and implementation.	Better design and implementation of policy instruments to achieve predetermined policy goals.
Government learning	How well administrative arrangements and processes have allowed policy implementation.	Members of the policy network, especially senior officials responsible for design and maintenance of policy processes.	Better design of administrative structures and processes within the bureaucratic systems (and engaging outside that system).
Social learning	How useful are our constructions of policies and goals.	Broader policy community, including both more and less closely engaged actors within and outside government.	Reframed problems and related goals, through changed cause-effect understanding or altered social preferences.
Political learning	How to most effectively engage with and influence political and policy processes.	Policy actors wishing to (a) change policy agendas and outcomes or (b) defend current agendas and outcomes.	Change in: problem definition; policy goals; and/or membership of the policy network.

Sources: Bennett and Howlett (1992); May (1992); Connor and Dovers (2004)

participatory policy regimes, these "safer" topics will often be addressed in processes that include interests from outside government who are committed to social and political learning.

Transferring policy lessons

Central to policy learning is the separation of information and lessons sought within and applicable within a single policy program or context, from that sought to be applied more generally within a policy domain or even to other domains. Learning within a program is necessary and useful, and more straightforward in terms of using the information and lessons gained. In environment and sustainability, there are often few completed policy experiments in a jurisdiction, so seeking lessons from as wide a possible catchment of policy experiences is necessary. Simple mimicry is not often appropriate in policy learning (May 1992), as cases are very rare where the problem, instruments and contexts are similar enough for a "blueprint" to be transferred unchanged from one situation to another. Two issues arise: the need for greater detail in identifying sources of insights and lessons; and the transferability of policy lessons across jurisdictions and sectors.

On the first issue, policy is composed of many parts. Learning from a policy experience through monitoring and evaluation can be focused on three general levels of detail:

- *Sub-program detail*: entailing examination and adaptation of specific lessons at the detail of specific elements of the policy process and program. For example, aspects of the monitoring program, participatory process or communication strategy used in one context that can inform policy design and implementation in another.

- *Policy program*: entailing a search for an overall package of elements that can be transferred to another situation.

- *Policy style*: entailing seeking more general ideas about different policy ideas that can be explored and tried elsewhere. For example, from another country which has tried self-regulatory rather than regulatory pollution control, or tradable rights rather than licensing in resource allocation.

Given that straight transfer is rarely appropriate, it can be proposed that the first and third levels are where useful policy learning can be achieved and where the suitability of transferring lessons to a different context can be dealt with best. Unfortunately, for reasons of haste and lack of resources and understanding, it is at the second or program level where transferable lessons are often sought – the tendency to grab a package of components from one context and transplant it somewhere else. The conceptualisation, design and implementation of new and innovative policies is more likely to arise from the exploration of different policy styles, matched with the selection and adaptation of a range of more specific insights and lessons from a range of sources, into a policy program carefully matched to the relevant context.

The second consideration is the transferability of lessons from one jurisdiction or sector to another. It makes clear sense to seek lessons widely, but care must be taken to ensure that the lessons are appropriate to the home problem context – "not to copy but to learn" (Rose 2005:1). In transferring lessons from one jurisdiction to another, there are no hard and fast rules. The key is to be clear about the basis of comparison and contrast, which may be: the use of similar policy instruments or strategies; the existence of similar political or legal systems; the similarity of social and economic settings; comparable resource availability or institutional capacity; or the substantive issues faced. For each, the information sought and the location of that information will vary, as will the form of learning (Table 8.2) being pursued.

Policy lessons can be sought across policy sectors or problems as well as across jurisdictions, both within and outside of the environment and sustainability domain. Within the domain, it is often the case that the organisation of government into separate sectors and departmental silos does not make cross-problem learning easy. The agencies and policy communities concerned with, say, nature conservation, water management, the forest estate and fisheries may have few connections, despite recent trends towards more integrated approaches to resource and environmental management. Yet each may be confronted by similar problem attributes (Chapter 3) or be using either similar or usefully contrasting strategies to attend specific stages and elements of the policy cycle, so that mutual learning is possible.

Outside the realm of resource and environmental management and into the broader sustainability domain, and even wider, policy learning can occur across unconnected areas of public policy. While great care should be taken with drawing policy lessons from widely different contexts, there is nonetheless significant scope if the instruction above regarding focusing on general policy ideas and very specific elements is followed, and the particular attributes of sustainability problems kept in mind. Problem attributes are a good guide to other policy sectors that may be useful areas for policy learning – *cognate policy sectors* – where similarities in the problems faced suggest that linkages may be fruitful. Obvious examples are emergency management, community development and public health, each of which also confronts pervasive uncertainty, extended temporal scales, strong demands for inclusive policy styles, and inter-jurisdictional connections.

The above paints policy monitoring, evaluation and the point of those activities – policy learning – as determined by a complex set of considerations. Policy learning is difficult and certainly necessary, and the ability of policy actors, networks and communities and society more broadly to engage in such learning will be determined by the extent to which the institutional system and organisational abilities within that system suit an adaptive, flexible, learning and yet purposeful approach to policy. That is the subject of the next two chapters.

Chapter 9

PARTICIPATION, TRANSPARENCY
AND ACCOUNTABILITY

General elements in policy processes
- Coordination and policy integration
- Public participation and community involvement
- Description and communication
- Transparency and accountability

This chapter sets out ways of ensuring that three "general elements" in the policy framework – public participation, transparency and accountability – can be addressed under different circumstances. The issues of coordination and integration are addressed in the next chapter due to their close relevance to institutional issues. More space is devoted to the issue of participation for two reasons: the increasing emphasis placed on participation in environment and sustainability; and the complexity of participatory policy regimes. Often, participation is considered mainly in terms of civil society participation in higher level politics, or of community involvement in local scale management activities. This chapter considers the issue at all levels in policy systems and all stages of the policy cycle.

Public participation

The idea that the public should be more involved in political and policy processes is widespread in modern societies, and in the environment and sustainability domain is particularly strong. However, the reasons for public participation in policy and the strategies available are not always clear. This chapter seeks to clarify this issue, by addressing: the logic of participation in policy; degrees of participation; what constitutes the public and community; and the different purposes and kinds of participation. For each, a categorisation or schema will be presented to provide a basis for finer resolution analysis of participatory approaches.

The logic of participation: how much is enough?

Participation in environment and sustainability policy is one entry point into larger issues of democracy, civil society and political power that are well beyond the scope of this book (for example, see Renn et al 1995; Healey 1997; Dryzek 2000; Munton 2003; Dobson 2003). There are a number of not mutually exclusive or unrelated reasons why either policy agencies or non-government interests would wish to see a greater involvement of the general public, interest groups or local communities in formulating and implementing policy and management:

- An ideological or political preference for participatory rather than more limited representative democracy, believing that it is appropriate for people to be involved in decisions that will affect their lives.

- Mistrust of governments by the public or interest groups, on the basis that governments alone cannot be trusted to act in the public or long-term interest. There is some evidence of a loss of trust in formal institutions in recent years.

- Experience with previous policy instruments such as straightforward regulation or simple public education campaigns, where one perceived reason for lack of policy success is the lack of involvement of affected parties.

- The increasing use of policy approaches that by their nature require close relationships between policy agencies and those outside government, such as community-based programs, market-based instruments, or more sophisticated educational or communicative processes involving two-way information flow.

- Recognition that local communities and other parts of the public possess perspectives and information that are valid and necessary for the design and implementation of policy and are not available from either government or expert advisers.

- Governments may favour more participatory approaches to allow cost-shifting through assigning responsibilities to local communities or production sectors consistent with a desire to reduce public expenditure.

In combination, these "logics" of participation produce a powerful imperative in environment and sustainability. Participatory policy and management is a rapidly evolving area of theory and practice, and the emphasis on debates and designs has changed over the years. An influential contribution was the "ladder of participation" developed by Arnstein (1969), which includes the following degrees of participation, or "rungs" on the ladder, where higher on the scale equals a greater level of citizen or public power:

- citizen control;
- delegated power;
- partnership;
- placation;
- consultation;
- informing;
- therapy;
- manipulation.

This schema deals with the *degree of participation*, or how much power is assigned, respectively, to government or to the populace. In the range of currently popular participatory options in environment and sustainability, the degree of power and responsibility assigned away from government varies greatly.

Many community-based programs are rather "top-down", where local groups are mechanisms for implementing the policies and decisions of government. Some instances of legal standing to object to developments or to policy decisions give citizens the power, through a court of law, to stop a government's actions. Many other instances evidence a mixture and a balance of assigned power.

As will be argued below, this variation is both expectable and desirable and the real issue is reasoned choice of different strategies across different contexts. However, five basic principles can be stated, informed by past experiences in participatory environmental management and the need to balance three imperatives: the empowerment of communities; the rightful responsibilities of governments; and the need for effective policy and management interventions. Participation, of whatever degree or kind, should be genuine, clear, sustained, flexible, and appropriately resourced:

- Whatever approach employed, the opportunities for participation should be *genuine*, and not offered simply to placate the public or to create the pretence of participation. If deciding to encourage participation, governments must accept that the input of members of the public or local community is a valid and potentially influential determinant of policy.

- Opportunities for participation should be *clear*, so that people within and outside of government are aware of the purpose, process, limits and duration. If the potential for public input to influence decisions has a limit this should be clear, or unrealistic expectations of influence will damage trust and thus both immediate outcomes and prospects of future partnerships.

- Participation should be *sustained*, rather than turned on and off at the convenience of government. The duration will depend on the nature of the problem/s being addressed, but given that most environment and sustainability problems operate over extended temporal scales, longerterm participatory processes will be the norm.

- Approaches to participation should be *flexible*, in two ways. First, at a given point in time, to allow participation by different interests in appropriate ways. Second, over time, by adjusting participatory options to suit evolving and changing policy problems and social expectations.

- Participation should be *appropriately resourced* if governments and others wish it to be effective and rewarding. Apart from the employed representatives of organised interest groups, public participation involves significant voluntary effort, and limits to such capacity may interfere with the quality of input as well as being inequitable. This issue is especially important for disadvantaged or remotely located individuals and groups. Resources may be financial, or the required assistance may be informational, administrative support, technical advice or time.

Some contemporary participatory structures and processes adhere to these principles well, however many do not.

The question of degree is a basic consideration in designing participatory approaches, and opinions will differ widely. Some people are impatient with participation and democracy, and would have governments make firm rules on the basis of expert advice and apply them without much consultation. Generally, though, such a policy style is not considered politically viable. Many advocates of participation either state or imply that more participation and citizen power is always better, although usually recognising the necessity for some form of central or overview judgment. However, there are three reasons why more is not necessarily better. First, there are many issues and problems, especially in environment and sustainability, where the broader public good or interests of future generations or of the environment demand some form of higher or central authority to balance or override local or short-term biases. Second, there are time and resource limits to the extent to which governments can consult and engage the public, when decisions need to be made soon. Third, there are limits to the "resource", that is the community's capacity to participate, balanced against the demands on peoples' time for work, family and other community commitments.

So, it is clearly the case that perfect participation is neither likely nor even desirable in many situations, and the issue of who is included becomes important.

Exclusion through inclusion

An overlooked aspect of an actively inclusive approach in policy or management is that the choice of a participatory strategy or form of participation will *include some people and exclude others*. For example, a catchment management policy including boards with community representatives could be organised over a variety of spatial scales. If established at river basin scale, a certain set of interests would be included, whereas at sub-catchment scale another set of more local interests would be relevant. Similarly, to define the scope of a participatory policy process dealing with river management as including water quality and salinity issues but not biodiversity will invite some people to take interest but implicitly exclude others. A representative role in a process that demands significant time and effort will disadvantage those without the capacity to make such a commitment. Or, a system of tradable resource rights may empower and engage only those with the interests and wherewithal to participate in the market, disenfranchising those with an interest in non-marketed assets.

Therefore – whether it is intended or not – inclusive approaches will often also be exclusive. This instructs careful thought as to the definition of the problem, and the purpose and kind of public participation and community involvement that will be enabled or encouraged. The next section identifies different purposes and kinds of participation. First, however, clarification of what the terms "public" and "community" mean in the context of environment and sustainability policy is offered, as the second of our categorisations to enable finer resolution analysis of what participatory design might be best utilised in a particular context. While terms such as "public" and "community" are used often, they conceal significant diversity.

The "public" and the "community"

In policy terms, the "public" is all those individuals within a jurisdiction affected by the public policy and decisions of the government. Many members of the public take little, no or only sporadic interest in policy, and in jurisdictions with voluntary voting do not even have that responsibility. The term "civil society" refers to the level of society between the general public and the state, made up of more organised groups who represent some defined interest and participate in political and policy debates. In the environment and sustainability domain, the term "community" is mostly used to denote place-based collections of people, such as the residents of a catchment or district, including those highly engaged with policy issues and those far less so.

To widen the definition of community away from only local communities, and to encourage a finer resolution in designing participatory strategies, Table 9.1 identifies the different "communities" relevant to resource and environmental management, that may wish to engage with different problems and require different participatory strategies for effective engagement. The defining feature of a "community" here is a *commonality of interest*.

There is overlap between some of the categories in Table 9.1, such as across professional and knowledge communities, or cultural and familial. The interest in environment and sustainability issues will vary across these communities, as will their level of organisation and capacity to engage in policy debate. Some communities – spatially defined or otherwise – are well organised, others are not. Some have a recognised and long-standing interest

Table 9.1: Defining "communities" in sustainability and environment

Type of community	Basis of common interest
Spatial (place-based)	Determined by affinity with or stake in the condition of a spatially defined natural or human system. The scale in this sense can vary enormously, from neighbourhood or rural district, through catchment and State or province, to the nation state.
Familial	Members of a located or extended family or kin network.
Cultural	Communities, possibly spatially defined but often not, linked by culture, ethnicity, religious belief, social ideology, etc.
Professional/workplace	Recognisable groups of people, often spatially dispersed, linked by profession or employment within a particular career type.
Knowledge/epistemic	Communities defined by a knowledge system, for example an academic discipline.
Economic/sectoral	Linked by economic interests, including dissimilar firms with collective placed-based economic interest or dispersed members of the same industry or commercial venture type.
Issue-related	Groups given identity and purpose by interest in or commitment to a substantive issue (eg species conservation, disabled access to buildings, specific health issues, etc).
Recreational	Groups linked through participation in or promotion of recreational activities (sporting groups, service clubs, etc).

in and influence on environmental policy whereas others find themselves on the periphery.

Obviously, people belong to multiple communities for different reasons, and usually the perspective and values brought to bear on a policy problem in environment and sustainability will be at least diverse, and often in conflict. For example, attitudes to proposals for change forest policy and management will vary enormously across the local timber-working community, forest industry association, bushwalking club, conservation society, ecological scientists, Indigenous owners and downstream irrigators.

The key rationale for participatory approaches is to identify, expose and hopefully reconcile such expectations and values.

The diversity of communities offers both challenges and opportunities to designing participatory policy approaches. The existence of often informal institutional arrangements supporting such communities represents an existing capacity for communicative and participatory activities (on the notion of social capital, see Baron et al 2000). However, these arrangements are often hard for an outsider to discern and work with, and vary from place to place.

A difficult issue in participatory approaches to policy is defining the degree of influence that different parts of "the community" should or will have in determining decisions or directions. Sometimes policy or legislation may define this, but very often government officials have to make judgments and no firm rules apply. In different situations, primacy may be given to those who live closest to some development or activity, to those with an economic interest, or to those with particular expertise. While in environmental law the issue of standing can be decided by a qualified court in accordance with established legal doctrines, in policy formulation and implementation the issue is less often clear. With any issue of substance, perfect agreement across different parts of the community is unlikely; a situation which on the one hand illustrates the inevitably political nature of many decisions and thus the need to recognise and allow for such higher level, integrative decisions to be made. On the other hand, it emphasises the need for methods that can incorporate diverse views in a transparent fashion, an issue discussed below and in the next chapter.

This diversity of definable communities within the broader community instructs that, depending on the nature of the problem at hand, different forms of participation opportunities will be required to engage different groups for a variety of purposes – the topic of the next section.

Purposes and kinds of participation

There is a political and moral argument for public participation in policy processes as inherently worthwhile. However, in practice there should be a clear idea of the purpose or purposes of participation, which will vary according to the problem faced and the matching array of interests and values, to allow choice of the most suitable participatory strategy. For example, in the case of an emerging issue, the key purpose of participation in the near term may be to allow inclusive debate over the nature of the problem and the threats or opportunities presented to different interests – that is, social debate (elements 1–2, Table 4.3). With a more familiar and well-defined problem, the main purpose may relate to implementing policy instruments or monitoring environmental conditions or management interventions (elements 3, 17–18). Table 9.2 identifies the main purposes of participation, with a short explanation and noting the primary elements of the policy framework to which each is relevant.

Table 9.2: The purposes of participation

Purpose	Explanation	Key elements in policy framework (Table 4.3)
Social debate	To allow debate about broader social values and goals	1-2
Policy formulation	To define policy problems, formulate policy or develop policy principles	8-11
Information and skills	To draw particular expertise or information into the policy process	3-5, 17-19
Policy implementation	To implement or aid implementation of policy instruments	12-13
Program delivery	To better deliver government policy program funds or government services	13-17
Management	To engage in management or on-ground works	13, 16, 18
Accountability	To ensure transparency and accountability in the policy process	All
Environmental monitoring	To monitor environmental conditions	3-4
Policy monitoring	To monitor and evaluate policy and management interventions.	17-19

Individuals and groups will see different purposes as more or less relevant to their interests and therefore as important, and will usually identify and pursue more than one purpose. Without clarity as to the purpose/s that are to be addressed via a participatory strategy, unrealistic expectations may exist and both the process and product of participation may disappoint. A strategy can serve multiple purposes if there is clarity around different ends and means. A public agency may be mostly interested in accountability in the acquittal of program funds, the engaged community group in local environmental conditions, and researchers in the generation of long-term data sets. The three priorities may be concurrently addressed and the outcomes satisfy all actors, given clarity in who is doing what and why.

Yet different purposes may not be achieved without implementing more than one participatory strategy, and there are many forms or kinds of strategy available (Table 9.3). This is a further illustration of the detail behind a broad policy instrument class (11 (community involvement) in Table 7.1, Chapter 7). The clarity argued for above demands a close match between the end (purpose) and the means to that end, the kind of strategy or process put in place. Obviously, with a number of different purposes, there is also a range of forms of participation available, including but not limited to the most familiar forms of engagement in a policy debate or in a local environmental management group. Table 9.3 sets out the more common forms.

Table 9.3: Forms of public participation and community involvement

As voters at different levels of government (national, State-provincial, local), whether compulsory or not depending on the jurisdiction.

As individuals via such mechanisms as letters to political representatives or newspapers, giving opinions on talk-back radio.

As members of *interest and pressure groups*, such as conservation organisations, farmer groups, political parties or consumer associations. The representativeness of these groups varies in terms of members' inputs into policies and priorities, and their voting power.

As consumers, through informed choice (eg mandatory labelling) and increasingly in a direct fashion as resource management regimes become marketised, where citizens become consumers (eg water, electricity).

As employees and workers in many industries, trades and professions implementing new environmental practices. A sharp division between work and not-work is blurred in this sense – someone practising recycling in the office is just as much a part of a community as they are when they recycle at home.

As recipients of information, including scientific information about environmental change, or messages about policy choices, changes or implementation.

As passive providers of information, acting as targets of researchers and policy analysts who will inform policy choices and policy design.

As active participants in research and monitoring projects in resource and environmental management that will inform policy (along a continuum from community leadership in research through to researcher or government control and direction). This may apply to gaining insights into environmental conditions, or into the success of policy or management interventions.

Through statutory rights such as freedom of information laws, rights to object in environmental planning and development control procedures, legal standing in courts or through environmental or social impact assessment.

Through mediation or conflict resolution processes run to allow debate and resolution of specific issues.

Through input to policy proposals or development approval processes such as government green or white papers, commissions of inquiry, parliamentary inquiries, etc.

Through representation in short-term policy processes run by governments, either individually or through representative groups, aimed at developing a widely supported policy on a specific issue or sector by engaging with interest groups and the public.

Through representation on advisory boards, committees, etc tasked with advising government on policy or management in a particular area (eg biodiversity conservation, forest management) or in a broader sense (eg a national council on sustainable development).

Through inclusion on statutory management boards or committees with a legal and administrative mandate and actual management function, such as a catchment management authority or management board of a national park.

Through participation in community-based monitoring groups and programs, whether community-led or government-sponsored or a combination of the two, targeting a specific issue and locality such as weeds or water quality.

As members of community-based groups engaged in resource and environmental management targeting a specific problem set in a particular locality (often in the form of "friends" or "care" groups)

In community-based or cooperative management arrangements (co-management), where actual management responsibilities are defined and devolved and a strong degree of local autonomy exists, e.g. a fishery or a multiple use reserve.

Via the use of deliberative and related *research and policy support methods*, such as opinion polling, citizens' juries or focus groups.

There is potential overlap between these forms, and the participatory strategy designed for a policy process will typically involve more than one, especially as the problem and response move through the policy cycle. Different forms of participation will be more relevant at different stages. There is considerable detail and variability in designing a specific strategy that cannot be discussed at length here. Key variables include the spatial scale, degree of autonomy and delegated responsibility, resourcing requirements, and administrative arrangements.

A crucial variable in many participatory designs revolves around *representativeness*. A pitfall in participatory approaches is that a sub-set of a community is engaged but does not adequately represent the range of interests. In higher level policy participation, it is often the case that a selected range of organised interest groups are regularly engaged in policy debates with government, rather than the general public – an approach referred to as corporatism. At times, this may be appropriate, whereas in other instances care should be taken to balance organised inputs with opportunities for more open debate via inquiries or deliberative techniques (see below). In more spatially-defined management contexts, except in very small communities, the equal inclusion of all individuals will be difficult. A system of representatives may be satisfactory, but another option is a mix of participatory options (see discussion of degrees of participation above) ranging from visibility of the process for the less interested to much closer engagement for those with key interests or more capacity for participation.

Where an ongoing, inclusive process or structure is to be established – such as a catchment management board or similar – the issue of democratic mandate emerges. Government appointees to management boards or advisory committees may or may not reflect the relevant communities or be viewed as representative by those communities. Governments face the choice of appointing specific individuals or allowing nominated interest groups to identify the representative. In some cases, use of existing institutional arrangements with a democratic basis, such as elected local governments, may be advisable.

Deliberative and related methods

There is a range of research and policy support methods that offer, in appropriate cases, more rigour and transparency in selecting and incorporating public or community input into policy. The general aim is to sample public knowledge and values, and to analyse these in a defensible fashion. This is a rapidly evolving area and many methods are contested and yet to be proven by widespread, repeated application.[1] Main examples of these methods include the following:

- Non-market valuation techniques that assign monetary value to non-traded environmental assets so that these can be incorporated into policy-making along with other economic measures of value. An example is contingent valuation, where a sample of citizens is surveyed to nominate an estimated monetary value of, for example, some threatened natural area, so as to provide an estimated value to compare with the economic value of proposed resource extraction.

- Broader scale surveys and opinion polls and more targeted focus groups to identify the distribution of public opinions and values around an environmental issue.

- A range of multi-criteria methods that offers a means to integrate multiple values and goals in a structured fashion, either towards deciding on optimal outcomes, or in a more heuristic fashion to facilitate discussion.

- Deliberative methods where information on and opportunities for structured discussion of an issue or problem is enabled amongst a representative sample of people. These approaches include large-scale consensus conferences, smaller citizens' juries, charettes and planning cells, and deliberative polls.

It must be stressed that many such methods attract significant criticism as to their methodological rigour and appropriateness for practical use, and should be carefully selected and used. The strength of such approaches is that the basis of the sample of the

---

[1] This discussion is extremely abbreviated. For a review see Munton (2003); Hajer and Wagenaar (2003); Fung and Wright (2003); for a summary description of many such methods, see the Citizen Science Toolbox at <http://www.coastal.crc.org.au>.

broader population is explicit, and in many cases the opinion or perspective gained is determined after provision of relevant information or through a process of deliberation, rather than a less informed, "off-the-cuff" opinion. A major constraint on the use of many of these methods is their cost – the expense of running a consensus conference would only be justified for major social issues, and at a finer scale few management agencies could afford to regularly utilise citizens' juries. Another problematic issue is the potential adverse reaction from previously closely engaged interest groups, who may feel disenfranchised by a reliance on methods which involve their replacement by samples of the wider population.

Returning to the idea of a "ladder" of participation, we can observe that more is not necessarily always better. Deliberative methods offer the ability to have public input in a potentially more rigorous and defensible manner but involving only a small number of people. However, such approaches may be viewed with suspicion by the unengaged public, and by interest groups who see this as circumventing their influence.

Recognising a wide range of participatory strategies to serve multiple purposes makes for a more complicated set of choices, but also a higher likelihood of policy and management advance and stakeholder satisfaction with the process and outcomes. With such a rich array of options, it will not always be the case that a person or group would wish to remain always on one rung of the ladder, but over time or across different issues to engage in policy and management in different ways as the problems and the responses change. Flexibility in participatory strategies is needed to allow people to move up and down the ladder, and indeed off and on the ladder. For many people, simply being able to know what is happening will be, at least for some of the time, quite sufficient. This means that, as well as active participation options, transparency is required.

Transparency and accountability

Creating the ability for the public to understand and observe processes of policy formulation and implementation is the most basic form of participation, and the entry point for closer engagement should the need emerge. Individuals or groups not closely engaged may in this way understand policy directions and be less likely to obstruct implementation. That is sufficient reason for close attention to be paid to elements 1 (social debate), 8 (problem definition) and 12 (communication) in the policy framework. *Transparency* in all stages of a policy process is thus a central principle for purely pragmatic reasons.

More generally, *accountability* is a fundamental principle in public policy and administration. Governments and non government participants in programs expend *public* resources. By definition the public, as citizens and taxpayers, has a right to know the basis and purpose of such investments. The exercise of statutory power by a responsible authority similarly involves the application of a public mandate as a representative of the people. In the case in environment and sustainability, many of the assets and values in question are common or public goods – air quality, wildlife, water resources, state-owned forests, and so on. This heightens the collective nature of costs and benefits and thus also the burden of accountability, as does the intergenerational dimension of sustainability.

The need for accountability is a matter of fundamental principle in politics and government but is not always dealt with well. Moreover, sustainability poses particular challenges compared with some other policy domains (Chapter 3). Extended spatial and temporal scales move consideration beyond political time frames and defined administrative jurisdictions, while ill-defined property and policy rights and multiple values create a complex mix of interest groups and audiences.

Familiar mechanisms for transparency and accountability in policy will often serve for sustainability, or may require some adjustment. Simply making information about policy decisions and their basis as widely available as possible is a sound and common strategy. That may be a matter of policy practice, or it may be formalised through legal requirement. The availability of legal challenges to decisions forms a backdrop to openness, as does the existence of freedom of information laws. Policy reviews by an independent auditor-general, commissioner of environment or national council for sustainable development, or through scrutiny by parliamentary committees, can serve to allow public input as well as opportunities for making decisions transparent and accountable. Linking environmental monitoring and policy monitoring (Chapters 5 and 8), especially through processes involving non-government groups, addresses information needs and policy learning as well as transparency and accountability and represents a major area requiring further development.

Transparency and accountability are prime antidotes to the emerging problem in modern systems of government of *declining trust* in public institutions. In a policy domain requiring long-term collaboration between government and non-government players such as sustainability, cynicism, erosion of trust, or even uncertainty as to why policy and management outcomes have not been satisfactory, represent serious risks. While there will be instances where secrecy or confidentiality may be warranted to protect privacy or commercial interests, this should be the exception rather than the norm. The implications for transparency and accountability of institutional reforms such as privatisation or outsourcing of public functions need careful consideration. Where cynicism on the part of the public exists, it does not take much apparent concealment of information for that cynicism to deepen. Participation, transparency and accountability are linked, and all are determinants of policy success and failure. Adherence to the guiding principles proposed earlier in this chapter – that participation should be genuine, clear, sustained, flexible, and appropriately resourced – should reduce the potential for loss of trust.

PART III

PROSPECTS FOR ENVIRONMENT AND SUSTAINABILITY POLICY

Chapter 10

COORDINATION, INTEGRATION, AND INSTITUTIONAL CHANGE

This chapter discusses three critical challenges that pervade environment and sustainability: policy coordination, policy integration, and institutional change. While these have been touched upon already they have not been confronted explicitly. The chapter deals with those *general elements* in the policy framework (Figure 4.2 and Table 4.3) not dealt with in the previous chapter, elements that serve to connect the policy process with the institutional setting that determines the direction and effectiveness of policy interventions. In the framework and in Chapter 2, the institutional general elements were summarised as five principles for adaptive institutions. These principles are not used to structure this chapter, as they have been addressed often enough along the way for ways of putting them into effect to be clear:

- *Persistence*: inherent in the reiterative, adaptive policy style advocated and through the policy cycle and framework, and more specifically see elements 3 and 17–20.
- *Purposefulness* of policy efforts, in terms of addressing understood goals: see elements 1, 8–11 and 13–16.
- *Information-richness* and information-sensitivity: see elements 3–4, 6 and 17.
- *Inclusiveness* of a wide range of values and interests: see elements 1–2, 14 and Chapter 9.
- *Flexibility* through mechanisms to enhance policy learning and improvement: inherent in the general approach to policy, and specifically elements 17–20.

The following discussion has bearing on implementing these principles, via a focus on three outstanding imperatives. Core to believable responses to environment and sustainability problems are clear provisions to coordinate policy across previously unconnected or fragmented sectors, the integration of ecological, social and economic concerns in policy, and to reform inappropriate institutional settings that are both the cause and the potential cure

161 *Which is most important in sustainable policy?*

of sustainability problems (see further Lenschow 2002; Lafferty 2004; Gibson et al 2005).

These three imperatives are tightly intertwined, but are used to divide the following into three parts. It is particularly problematic to separate policy coordination and policy integration. Here, *policy coordination* refers to institutional and organisational structures and process that better connect previously separate parts of the policy system. *Policy integration* refers to the joint analysis of ecological, social and economic concerns within the policy process.

Central to the three matters dealt with here is the inescapable fact that, due to the nature of institutional change, emerging and significant social concerns such as sustainability will be largely addressed through institutional settings that have evolved in the past in response to other social concerns and goals. Institutionally, we are prisoners of history. Positively, such inherited institutional settings evolved and became embedded for often good reasons and are resistant to change, providing predictability and performance in public affairs and social transactions. Negatively, we may be trapped into modes of thinking and acting that are not suited to evolving problems. For example, the division of responsibility for public policy into specialised portfolios and agencies has had many benefits in efficiency and purpose – the point of specialisation. Yet for responding to sustainability, such specialised agencies can operate as "silos", preventing cross-sectoral and cross-problem responses. Likewise, a hierarchy of levels of government can allow public functions to be undertaken at the optimal scale, but can also render it difficult to address sustainability problems that span political and administrative boundaries.

Following the style of the book, this chapter offers a mix of general discussion of the nature of the policy and institutional challenges, along with some frameworks and checklists to guide thinking, analysis and choice of strategies. The three issues covered are complex, significant and long term, and the following is introductory rather than prescriptive or definitive. The complexity of institutional systems and of policy processes is such that multiple options exist for multiple purposes – some existing institutional structures will require redirection or refocusing whereas others will require radical change. The aim here is to offer ways in which decisions about appropriate strategies can be more informed and structured, according to the particular problem context and practical possibilities for institutional change.

The balance between substantial institutional change and utilising existing arrangements warrants close consideration. In some situations the opportunity for substantial change exists – where the "policy window" is wide open and the problems widely accepted as serious. At other times, the context will be such that only incremental change can be entertained. However serious one believes environment and sustainability problems are, it is not the case that bigger policy and institutional change is always better: existing capacities may be more effective if properly used. It may be that creating a new institution or organisation, or radical reform of an existing one, achieves little despite the intended appearance of positive change. As with policy instruments, the institutional strategy should be viewed as a means to an end, not an end to be advocated for its own sake.

A central tension in institutional change for sustainability revolves around the idea of "goodness of fit", which suggests that a characteristic of successful (that is, influential, long-lived) institutions is whether they fit in their operating environment.[1] This makes sense, but for sustainability, where the operating environment (that is, institutional system) is part of the problem, then sufficient fit is likely to equal insufficient change. Thus institutional reform options need to be achievable in a political sense (that is, to fit), while at the same time be capable of driving significant change (that is, not to fit, to unsettle). The options and principles explored below can be viewed against that tension.

Policy coordination across sectors and jurisdictions

Environment and sustainability problems show little respect for the political and administrative boundaries within which public policy is structured in modern societies. Coordination of information, communication and policy formulation and implementation across political portfolios, policy sectors and jurisdictions is required and, despite many initiatives in recent years, policy coordination for

---

1   For a discussion of this and other characteristics of successful institutions in a general sense, as opposed to in the specific context of environment and sustainability, see Goodin (1996).

sustainability remains an uncertain art. Recalling the complexity and multiple layers of function and responsibility within the landscape of public policy (Table 2.2), coordination is no small task. Coordination is required for most policy domains (for example, health, welfare, education, and so on), and many of the options for environment and sustainability are the same as have been tried and tested in other areas (on coordination and other contemporary trends in public administration, see Christensen and Lægreid 2002; McLaughlin et al 2002). However, the task is especially hard as the span of policy sectors and of jurisdictions of relevance to sustainability is arguably wider than for other domains, and as there is a wider range of spatial and temporal scales across which problems operate.

Two simple categorisations can help to inform understanding of the coordination task and selection and design of options. The first identifies the imperative – the purpose or *kind* of coordination:

- *Intra-jurisdictional*, to increase coordination across port-folios and policy sectors within a jurisdiction, addressing the principle of policy integration through organisational or institutional change. This applies within the resource and environmental area (for example, connecting water and forest management, or coastal planning and oceans policy), or across more distant sectors (connecting environment and social or economic policy).

- *Inter-jurisdictional*, to increase coordination across the political and administrative boundaries that define jurisdictions. This may be *vertical* coordination, such as to connect national and state or provincial government policy processes, or state or provincial and local government. Or it may be *horizontal* coordination, to connect policy processes across similar levels of government (more than one nation state, multiples states or provinces, multiple local governments).

- *Creating new jurisdiction or spatial scale*, either inter- and/or intra-jurisdictional, where the mismatch between existing boundaries and scales of policy and administration and the problems being addressed are perceived to be serious enough to warrant the creation of a new spatial scale of policy or administrative competence defined by natural systems function (for example, catchments) or cultural or socio-economic variables (for example, Indigenous lands or resource extraction systems).

The second categorisation addresses the *degree* of coordination required, in terms of extent and longevity needed relative to the problem or problems to be addressed:

- *Extent of coordination*: to (a) establish informational or functional linkages across sectors or jurisdictions but where existing organisational entities remain; or (b) establish substantially new organisational or institutional entities that incorporate all or part of the functions of existing ones.

- *Longevity of coordination*: involving (a) short-term problems or tasks addressed through policy processes or activities over a defined time period; or (b) establishment of linkages or new structures of an ongoing nature.

A final consideration is whether policy coordination will be undertaken primarily within government, involving existing patterns of inclusion of non-government policy actors, or whether new or extended forms of multi-stakeholder structures and functions are warranted to enhance connectivity across policy sectors (see further Chapter 9).

The above typology is generalised and somewhat loose. The choice of the optimal strategy in a given situation will require more detail and likely reflect a combination of both kind and degree of coordination. However, it offers an initial means for ensuring clarity about what is required. Using these informing perspectives, specific options can be considered. Table 10.1 summarises some main policy and institutional options for policy coordination in environment and sustainability.

All the options identified in Table 10.1 are valid under different circumstances, and to address environment and sustainability properly a number of options would be required within or across any jurisdiction. Investing too much hope in a single mechanism is unwise, as although interrelated, different options address different needs. For example, a commissioner for environment residing in a central agency or answering to the legislature is one way of forcing multiple policy sectors and agencies to attend to and report on sustainability dimensions within their realm of responsibility. That is an in-government function, even with strong communication to the public. An inclusive national council for sustainable development or similar body attends some of the same needs, but incorporating interests beyond government to drive policy debate.

Table 10.1: Options for policy coordination

General form of coordination	Major options (selected)
Policy processes	Overarching environment and/or sustainability policy, or policy development defined by problems that traverse policy sectors (eg oceans, biodiversity, energy, etc).
	Policy assessment processes: strategic environmental assessment; sustainability assessment; regulatory impact review; environmental risk assessment.
	Legislative review for consistency with sustainability principles.
	Insertion of environment and sustainability consideration in agency decision-making through statutory expression of sustainability principles.
	Agency reporting on environment and/or sustainability (including triple bottom line accounting).
Inter-agency and cross-sectoral (within jurisdiction)	Connecting existing parts: cabinet review processes; ministerial councils, inter-departmental committees or taskforces; joint policy programs; information sharing; parliamentary committees.
	Merging wholes or parts: portfolio and agency re-organisation (super ministries, mergers, etc).
	Whole-of-government mechanisms: offices or commissioners of environment or sustainability; councils for sustainability; sustainability legislation.
Inter-government (across jurisdictions)	Horizontal: ministerial councils, intergovernmental agreements; joint policy programs; information sharing; intergovernmental agencies; accreditation of standards and processes; joint functions across local government.
	Vertical: ministerial councils; intergovernmental agreements; delineation and/or clarification of responsibilities; joint programs; accreditation and standardisation; information sharing; joint management bodies; taskforces; complementary legislation.
Multi-stakeholder	Incorporation of a wider range of non-government policy actors from different policy communities to enable coordination of ecological, environment and social concerns in:
	o Social debate and policy formulation (eg inclusive National Councils for Sustainable Development; stakeholder roundtables, etc); or
	o Policy implementation and management activities (eg inclusive catchment management bodies; regional environment and development boards, etc).

A strategic environmental assessment regime is another, related but different strategy, and one that may be used in concert with the previous two. (These options are discussed further below.)

Scale and subsidiarity

Intergovernmental coordination is a particular challenge in sustainability, in great part because governments guard their power jealously. The level of nation states and international policy is one not dealt with in any detail in this book for reasons of space and focus, but is of course crucially important to sustainability (see Chasek 2000; Stokke and Thommessen 2001; Speth 2003). But the resistance to and difficulty of sharing or transferring power are often no less within one nation state, most especially in federal systems of government. Many of the options above offer a way forward on this, but remain in practice retarded by territoriality and jealousy over power. In recent years the concept of *subsidiarity* has emerged, especially in Europe, around which consideration of the delineation of powers can be more fruitfully discussed. Subsidiarity instructs that responsibility should be located at the lowest level of government in terms of effectiveness and appropriateness for the function in question.[2] That invites careful analysis of the policy problem faced, and then of the best locus of responsibility for formulating and managing the policy response. It may be that policy formulation and implementation are assigned to different levels, and with sustainability as a multi-scale problem set it will rarely be that one level can operate in isolation from either other levels or from other parts of society. Nonetheless, subsidiarity as a guiding principle forces attention on the appropriateness of the location of power and responsibility with reference to the problem context rather than only political considerations.

It is worth ensuring clarity about the scales over which policy and institutional responses might be mounted. While the following revisits the above discussion, the issue of spatial scale is deeply recurrent in sustainability and deserves close attention. While it is generally accepted that management, policy and institutional reform needs to occur at multiple scales, and must involve ongoing

---

2   Subsidiarity does not suggest simply devolving responsibility to the lowest level of government possible, as is sometimes suggested by, alternatively, lower levels of government wishing for greater power, or higher levels wishing to abrogate irksome policy tasks through devolution.

coordination across scales, the full range of available spatial/administrative scales is not always acknowledged in discussion either of the larger sustainability challenge or in the context of specific problems. Some discussions concentrate on the basic levels of government (for example, national, state, local), whereas others less favourable to the idea of government as leader concentrate on other scales or bases of human organisation, governance or natural system function. Other discussions again are framed around quite different bases for policy and institutional development, cutting across spatial-administrative scales. The following seeks to capture this range, including non-spatial bases for policy and institutional reform:

- *Supra-national*, being intergovernmental constellations including international (for example, the United Nations), multi-lateral and bilateral, "regional" organisations of government, trade zones, and various groupings of nation states (for example, Group of Eight (G8), Organisation for Economic Cooperation and Development (OECD)), and groupings of commercial interests or NGOs across similar scales.

- The *nation state*, which is the primary location of legal competency and the point of coordination with supra-national processes and law, and between those and sub-national policy and processes.

- *Formal (legally-competent) sub-national*, including State, provincial and territorial governments, local governments, and in some cases other formal layers of government (the powers and capacities of these vary significantly between countries). Sub-national governments may create cross-jurisdictional bodies that enjoy legal competence, such as joint management authorities or regional organisations of local governments).

- *Less formal or non-traditional sub-national* scales, such as regional, bioregional or catchment, where policy and management are increasingly being framed but which typically lack legal competence, a statutory base or independence of resourcing or activity. Also increasingly common is the *locale or district scale* and the analogous neighbourhood scale in urban areas at which most community-based initiatives operate.

- *Household, land parcel, firm,* and so on, that are the fundamental social, legal and economic loci of much human responsibility and activity, and underpin the logic of many policy interventions that seek to influence human behaviour. The *individual* scale exists below these and is highly relevant to policy options based on communicative or economic rationalities.

- A large range of *non-spatial "scales"*, or loci of policy responsibility or human activity, including: resource sectors, firm type or industry category, environmental issue, demographic stratum, language or cultural group, communities of advocacy or interest, professions, and so on. Many policies are made and implemented with the primary focus on such loci or concerns, within a particular spatial-administrative scale.

The issue of *legal competence* is crucial, given the key role played in institutional systems by the rule of law.[3] Too often, encouraging initiatives at non-traditional scales of policy and governance (for example, regions, catchments, locales) have been unsupported by legal competence, as well as administrative capacity and other resources, and have been short lived and less effective than they might have been.

Commonly, policy or institutional reforms and arrangements involve more than one, and usually more than two, of the above scales, and a mixture of spatial-administrative and non-spatial scales (for example, coordinated local and State government action on a widely dispersed but nodal economic activity with particular environmental or social implications). That is, the logic of a policy intervention is to address, most often, a non-spatial process or phenomenon, not the jurisdictional basis for doing so, no matter how deeply ingrained or powerful the jurisdictional rationale is. Government as a means, not as an end in itself.

The range of scales outlined above offer the basis for matching the scale/s for organising a policy or institutional response, matched against the capacities and detail of the political context, and the nature of the problem being addressed. The approach to problem definition outlined in Chapter 5 (element 8) is

---

3   In modern resource and environmental management, statute law is the usual basis of competence, and to a lesser or indirect extent common law. In some contexts, such as Indigenous land management, customary law or other informal cultural institutions may be the basis of authority and competence.

scale dependent – one jurisdictional scale sees a macro-problem, another sees a micro-problem. Bringing scale, problem and institutional setting together provides a basis for working through the issue of subsidiarity.

In part these options will further the prospects for implementing the principle of policy integration, but even with organisational and institutional changes put in place to encourage and create the capacity for integration, procedures and methods for integration in support of policy decisions will be required in specific situations.

Policy integration methods: Ecological, social and economic

The policy, organisational and institutional strategies surveyed above address coordination, and go some way to enabling policy integration. A sharper focus on policy integration reveals the need for operational methods and approaches to support policy-making that integrates environmental, social and economic information and considerations. This may be done within more coordinated or new organisational structures, or within existing, less connected locations in the policy system. While central to sustainability, there is little consensus in theory or in practice on how policy integration can best occur. This is not surprising: the task has only quite recently been defined, and involves incorporating very different rationalities and forms of information into the policy process. This section identifies major policy integration methods, recognising that a range of options exist and are valid under different circumstances, and comments briefly on issues to do with their implementation. Table 10.2 identifies major available options under four broad (and not completely impermeable) categories: economic and neo-economic; integrated modelling; policy assessment; and discursive methods.

Table 10.2 suggests a range and diversity of possible approaches, none of which are uncontested or suitable across the board, but which collectively offer a rich menu of possibilities to operationalise the policy integration principle in a manner suitable for the problem at hand. Within each method or approach, there is considerable actual and potential scope for variation in application. Strategic environmental assessment is a procedure that may utilise various methods itself, and will require legal, administrative and institutional settings. Multi-criteria analysis may seek a single, optimal

Table 10.2: Methods for policy integration (selected)

Category	Main examples
1. Economic/ neo-economic	Extended cost-benefit analyses (incorporating values not measured economically in traditional cost-benefit analyses); non-market valuation (eg contingent valuation, hedonic pricing, travel cost method); choice modelling; multi-criteria analysis; natural resource accounting; agent-based modelling (Common 1995; Garrod and Willis 1999).[4]
2. Integrated assessment and modelling	Various forms of bio-economic and related modelling, sometimes including agent-based models and scenario modelling (Jakeman and Letcher 2003).
3. Policy assessment methods and procedures	Strategic environmental assessment, sustainability assessment and integrated policy assessment, extending assessment of proposals beyond the project scale of environmental impact assessment to the assessment of policies, plans and programs in non-environmental policy sectors (Partidario and Clark 2000; Marsden and Dovers 2002; Gibson et al 2005).
4. Discursive approaches	Planning cells, collaborative planning, citizens' juries, consensus conferences, and a range of inclusive approaches (see Chapter 9) (Elster 1998; Munton 2002).

outcome, or it may be heuristic and seek rather to inform discussions. Likewise, considerable variation and flexibility is offered by various modelling approaches. However, few of these have been widely or influentially implemented, due to the recent emergence of the methods and the problems they address, but also to the fact that some at least have no obvious location within the institutional system and/or pose inherently disturbing challenges to existing powers and interests within that system. That issue is revisited in the last part of this chapter.

Bringing together two previous discussions, the question arises of deciding which institutional strategy or policy support method to use at different scales. Using some examples of key principles from Chapters 3 and 6 (see Table 6.1) as well as options

---

4   In this rapidly evolving area, and generally across environmental policy, a thorough annual coverage is available through the *International Yearbook of Environmental and Resource Economics*, published annually by Edward Elgar Publishing.

above, the following illustrates the match of coordination or integration option with the scale or scales at which they would logically be implemented.

1. *Policy integration principle* (principle 4, Table 6.1):

   - Strategic environmental assessment (SEA). Largely, it will be national or state/provincial governments that have the legal competence, breadth of policy responsibilities and administrative capacity to implement SEA.

   - Portfolio and agency redesign within public bureaucracies, either locating responsibility for sustainability in a central location (for example, office or commissioner for sustainable development), or organisation of larger portfolios and departments that incorporate a wider range of policy responsibilities than simply "environment". This strategy is clearly relevant mostly to national and state government. Note that it is argued by some that such reorganisation is unnecessary in local government, given the small size and thus non-fragmentary nature of such bodies.

   - National Councils for Sustainable Development (NCSD), of which over 70 believable ones have been created, aimed at inclusion of non-government interests into the policy process, but also to bring environmental, social and economic interests together. Seen by some as a domestic equivalent of the UN Commission on Sustainable Development, by nature these are most relevant at the national scale, but equivalents (for example, sustainability round-tables) have been established at state/provincial level as well.

   - Statutory expression of sustainability principles to be considered in policy formulation and decision-making across policy sectors. This is a role of national and legally-competent sub-national governments.

2. *Precautionary principle* (principle 7, Table 6.1):

   - Statutory expression – as above, this is the responsibility of national and sub-national governments with the power to enact legislation. The non-binding expression of the precautionary principle might be made at other levels, such as by local government or industry groups.

- Implementation – taking account of the precautionary principle in decision-making is relevant at all decision-making scales where it is expressed as a guiding principle, in both policy and law, utilising a range of methods (see Chapter 5).

3. *Community involvement* (principle 9, Table 6.1) is again context-dependent with respect to the appropriate spatial or government scale, as the following examples illustrate (Chapter 9):

   - Ongoing participatory policy formulation processes are generally more suited to higher levels of government, and broader spatial scales (noting that community inputs to local government are deemed by many to be an inherent feature of that institution).
   - Practical participation in environmental management is generally deemed best driven at local scale, even if enabled and even held accountable at higher levels.

4. *Policy innovation* (principle 10, Table 6.1), is highly context-dependent, with different instruments being suitable at various policy scales, often in a coordinated fashion (or at least a top-down fashion), for example:

   - Most market mechanisms (tradable resource rights, taxation measures, and so on) will be implemented by higher level governments with the necessary legislative power and span of responsibility and influence. However, a rate rebate scheme may well be implemented at local government scale.
   - Educative instruments can be implemented by any level of government or scale of participatory governance. Generally, more specific and practical educative strategies will be best suited locally, whereas generic (and potentially systemic) curriculum change or public education would be formulated at a higher level.

There is not usually a single appropriate scale at which these options should be implemented. Typically they can and should be implemented across multiple, interdependent scales and the choice will be dependent on the specific problem being addressed and on the particular legal, political, social and environmental context. Moreover, cross-scale coordination is not simply optimal but essential. If one scale of purpose or implementation fails, then the entire interdependent policy or institutional strategy may also fail. This raises the question of deeper institutional change and the way in which it can be understood.

Institutional change for sustainability

There are limits to what policy change and organisational reform can achieve in the absence of more substantial institutional reform. Environment and sustainability policy as presented in this book involves many relatively easy improvements in information use and procedures in policy-making. Although they add up to a significant body of endeavour, the components of that endeavour mostly are not frightening and may even seem commonsense. However, progress is widely perceived as insufficient, in part because of unsuitable institutional settings within which these more immediate policy and organisational initiatives have been undertaken. This section deals with this issue of longer-term institutional change, following the view expressed by the World Commission for Environment and Development (WCED 1987: 9):

> The real world of interlocked economic and ecological systems will not change; the policies and institutions concerned must.

To explore the nature of institutions and institutional change, it is worth being clear about the subject, by revisiting the definitions provided in Chapter 1:

- *Institutions* are persistent, predictable arrangements, laws, processes or customs serving to structure political, social, cultural or economic transactions and relationships in a society. They may be informal or formal, and allow organised, collective efforts around common concerns. Although persistent, institutions constantly evolve.

- The term *institutional system* conveys the fact that it can be limiting to concentrate on single institutions. Institutions are embedded in complex, interactive systems of many institutions, organisations and actors, and in understanding social and policy change this interdependency must be taken into account.

- *Organisations* are manifestations of institutions, such as specific departments, associations, agencies, and so on. In some cases, an organisation may be persistent, recognisable and influential enough to be regarded as an institution, but generally organisations can be more quickly dissolved or radically changed whereas an institution is more durable.

Policy processes and interventions, the information flows used and a range of policy actors all operate within *institutional systems*, and these systems are complex and often resistant to change. That resistance or resilience is a function of the durable nature of institutions, but also of their complexity – efforts toward institutional change are often absorbed without seeming effect amidst this complexity. That said, institutions can change rapidly, in response to sudden imperatives or to slower build up of pressure over time (recall the discussion of "policy windows" in Chapter 2). So, institutional change is normally slow, occasionally swift, and often uneven over time. Policy interventions of a marginal nature, but of substance and involving new problems and information, may drive change in the institutional system over time, by familiarising actors in those institutions with new information and constructions of problems.

Resilience in the face of pressures for change can be either a positive or negative characteristic. The following is a simple characterisation of different forms of institutional resilience (Handmer and Dovers 1996):

- *Type 1 resilience: Resistance and maintenance.* Positively characterised by purpose and stability, optimisation of resource use, and a low risk of ill-considered decisions. Negatively characterised by denial of or resistance to change, appeals to ignorance, and awaiting crisis before entertaining reform of operating assumptions and normal practices.

- *Type 2 resilience: Change at the margins.* Positively characterised by admission of need for change, well-considered reactions to outside pressures and new situations, and manageable, incremental responses. Negatively characterised by inability to cope with major shifts in operating environment or new knowledge, addressing symptoms rather than causes, lack of long-term strategy, and danger of masking continuation of problems through a veneer of change.

- *Type 3 resilience: Openness and adaptability.* Positively characterised by recognition of uncertainty and imperatives for change (including underlying causes), and by preparedness to adapt quickly. Negatively characterised by inefficiency and possible maladaptation through ill-informed change.

All three are appropriate depending on the circumstances; that is, the problem faced, state of knowledge and implications of not taking action. In the case of environment and sustainability, advocates of urgent change would view Type 1 as wrong and Type 3 as more advisable and even urgently required. Those not convinced that there is a sustainability problem would regard Type 1 as sensible, and Type 3 as unnecessary and dangerous. In general, institutional responses to sustainability thus far would fall in the range of Types 1–2.

If institutions are the basic rules of society and are the means whereby we manage our social and economic transactions, then institutional change is a serious business. Recalling the multiple design variables of institutions (Table 7.4), and recognising individual institutions as parts of complex, dynamic institutional systems, it is also a very complex business. The task facing one group in society who believes that a particular social goal – for example, environment and sustainability – deserves to be more strongly represented in the institutional landscape is never quick and easy. Pragmatically, the most viable strategy is to seek to embed the social goal in the institutional system in a manner acceptable to the prevailing political and social value set, but in such a manner as to open the way for longer-term reorientation in multiple parts of the system.

To explore this further, we can briefly consider four institutional strategies that have – potentially at least – significant ability to disturb and reshape the institutional system over time. There are more revolutionary options available, such as major constitutional renewal or reform of the structure and logic of government, but in keeping with the tone of the book we will consider options that are purposeful and potentially transformative over the long term, but incremental and still realistic. The four are: legal change through legislative review and statutory expression of principles; a strategic environmental assessment regime; inclusive national councils for sustainability; and an in-government commissioner for environment or sustainability.[5]

1. *Legislative review and statutory expression of sustainability principles*. The broad body of statute law pervades policy-making through the definition of process and statement of rules. Policy agencies' objectives are set through enabling statutes, as are what are held to be important considerations and the rights and responsibilities for decision-making (including public participation). Statute law reflects social concerns, and takes on new concerns as these strengthen and legislatures react to changing social values. There has been widespread legal expression of traditional environmental protection in law, but many regard this as not very effective, and the expression of sustainability principles has tended to be (a) relatively weak and discretionary in terms of instructing decision-makers in non-environmental policy sectors, and (b) vague in terms of instructing decision-makers on how to interpret these principles. Statutory expression of sustainability principles (Tables 3.3 and 6.1) across major policy sectors (that is, economic, transport, energy, planning, trade, finance, and so on) is a logical step toward embedding the idea in institutional systems, and rather than in an ad hoc fashion could be done purposefully. A wide-ranging legislative review would seek to identify (a) statutory provisions that are barriers to progressing sustainability (for example, perverse incentives) and (b) areas where the insertion of sustainability principles as statutory objects would serve to embed these considerations in significant policy processes. The impact of such expression would not be swift, but would over time drive a shift in the logic of policy-making. The prospects for such a review would vary across jurisdictions, but in any would be a significant move of sustainability from the margins to the core of policy. As such, considerable opposition would be expected.

2. *Strategic environmental assessment (SEA)*. Strategic Environment Assessment incorporates an assessment of environmental implications into policy and program development in non-environmental sectors. The logic is that project-level environment assessment, while important and necessary, is: reactive;

---

5   For more detailed discussion of these see Dovers (2002); Connor and Dovers (2004).

does not handle cumulative impacts across developments; and most importantly, does not attend indirect causes of environmental degradation that lie within the institutional system. With a change of focus, SEA may be evolved into a more integrative sustainability assessment. Although the best-known, promoted and understood strategy for policy integration, and a statutory provision in a range of countries for up to 30 years, the practice and impact of SEA has been slight. This is a result of a lack of understanding of how to undertake assessments, but more of a lack of preparedness on the part of governments to implement what is largely a discretionary form of scrutiny of their own policy directions and processes. Until recent embedding of SEA more substantially in the European Union, the prospects for SEA appeared weak, and still remain uncertain.

3. *National Councils for Sustainable Development (NCSD)*. Since the idea was first promoted in 1992, NCSDs or equivalent bodies have been created in some 70 countries to provide a multi-stakeholder forum at the national level to promote sustainability. (Increasingly, state and provincial governments are creating similar bodies.) They vary from poorly supported advisory bodies through to more permanent, better resourced bodies with defined functions. The functions range from policy discourse and research, to advice to government, reporting on international obligations, and independent carriage of policy processes and social debate. Most, however, are marginal if nonetheless useful players, often crippled by insufficient resources, unclear mandates and poor connections to others parts of the policy process. Conceivably, NCSDs offer potential as a site for what many believe is required: a more inclusive form of governance for environment and sustainability where more substantial powers are vested in more inclusive bodies (for example, public reporting on government policy implementation, legislative review, or independent oversight of strategic assessment). No NCSD or any similar body has such power yet, and although once again opposition would be significant, it is not an unimaginable evolution of their present status within normal political parameters.

4. *Commissioner for or office of environment or sustainability*. Many jurisdictions have created some form of whole-of-government mechanism to oversee policy development and coordination for environment and sustainability, with the focus varying

from a strictly environmental focus to a broader focus on sustainability. Some take the form of a semi-independent commissioner with supporting staff; others a policy office or unit within a central agency (for example, planning agency, prime minister or premier's department). The basic intent is to provide advice to government and promote sustainability considerations across policy sectors, portfolios and agencies. Other functions include public education, research strategies, state of environment reporting, and assessment of agency performance (although rarely equating to an SEA regime). Although largely a within-government mechanism, there is typically a public reporting and stakeholder engagement dimension. (In some jurisdictions, a Cabinet level committee has the role, however given the confidential nature of Cabinet proceedings this is a very exclusive mechanism.) The commissioner/office option complements but does not replace the NCSD or similar – the former is a government rather than a governance strategy. Although now widespread, commissioners and offices often are poorly resourced relative to the size of the task, which is to embed a new and complex social and policy goal and methods for its implementation across parts of the institutional system unfamiliar with the goal and possibly even hostile to it.

The key factor for many in such situations is obvious: environment and sustainability, although strongly supported in policy rhetoric, is but one social and policy goal amidst many, and moreover one that does not have the same priority of longer-standing social and economic concerns. The response to that reality cannot only be to state the new social goal more loudly and persistently, but to examine strategies for inserting it into the institutional system and policy process, and in the minds of policy actors, in ways that create the conditions for familiarity, learning and expertise to evolve. The four options above, and other options and frameworks discussed elsewhere in this book, fit this description.

These situations – where the option is understood but not yet evident, or is evident but marginal in power – emphasise the discussion at the start of this chapter about the balance between fitting in to the institutional system and thus not changing it, and being such an ill-fit that the option is not politically feasible. Deeper reforms of this sort are unlikely to be achieved quickly, as the slow evolution and still uncertain status of SEA demonstrates.

Therein lies a paradox: policy networks may be reluctant to implement something until they are familiar with it, but familiarity comes with implementation. Significant policy change involves cultural change within persistent institutions and knowledge systems. These change slowly and this frustrates people in and outside of government who believe environment and sustainability to be important and urgent. The current era is a transition phase that is likely to persist for some time. Understanding that significant institutional change requires ongoing effort and maintenance can be helped by recognition of some overarching principles.

Principles for institutional change

The guiding principles presented below are those derived from examination of several case studies of institutional change for sustainable development.[6] The seven principles are organised under two broad categories: problem (re)framing, and (re)organising government. These two categories reflect the need to understand sustainability problems in all their peculiarity and complexity, and to refashion the structures and functions of government to handle these problems better. The nature of the sustainability problem is such that it is not possible to cleanly separate either these two categories or the principles developed under them: they are strongly interrelated. The following is a sharp summary:

1. **Problem (re)framing,** relevant to the formation of a shared and coherent social construction of the sustainability problem:
   - *The institutional accommodation of the sustainability discourse –* recognising that sustainability is a new, complex and contested idea that is not fully understood or endorsed in policy communities and the wider population. Such understanding is a long-term project, and thus an ongoing discourse around the idea is required and needs to be encouraged and maintained by (not only but especially) governments through creation and maintenance of conducive institutional arrangements and persistent discursive, policy-oriented networks.

---

6   See Connor and Dovers (2004). The case studies were European environmental policy, New Zealand's *Resource Management Act*, National Councils for Sustainable Development, strategic environmental assessment, and property rights instruments.

- *The role of normative change* – advancing policy and institutional change for sustainability begs the acceptance of this strategy as necessary and valid by a sufficiently large group within the populace, which implies widespread normative change. If proposals for substantial institutional change are inconsistent with community norms, successful reform is unlikely. This principle instructs proponents to be aware that institutional and normative change are interdependent, and to build that recognition into policy processes (that is, connect element 1 with later elements in the policy cycle).

- *The role of legal change* – recognising that the law (constitutional documents, statutes, common law) are crucial to more profound institutional change, and that proposals for reform must incorporate an agenda of supportive or at least not obstructive legal change. Crucial to this are statutory expression of sustainability principles (especially precaution and policy integration) and an intentional strategy for developing understanding of their meaning and implementation.

- *International law and policy and drivers* – recognising that the international level of political discussion has driven the sustainability policy agenda. However, more recently the interaction between the supra-national and national scales has been crucial to the maintenance of the agenda, communication of experiences in institutional change, and to allowing the comparison between nations who are leading and those more reluctant to change that is so valuable in enlivening debate in the latter.

2. **(Re)organising government**, to embed the organisational logic of sustainability in the landscape of public policy and organisations:

    - *Integration in policy and practice* – recognising that integration (ecological, social, economic) is crucial to the sustainability idea, and requires purposeful and sustained development of policy processes and standards for it to occur (for example, through structural reform of government, law reform, SEA, methodological development, and so on).

- *Subsidiarity*, recognising that policy responsibility should reside, and decisions should be taken, at the most effective and appropriate level, for reasons that are political (democratic), administrative (economies of scale) and substantive (the nature of sustainability problems). With sustainability, where most issues must be handled at multiple scales, this demands flexible implementation of subsidiarity.

- *Reiteration*, recognising that sustainability is a long-term social and policy project being launched in the face of considerable uncertainty about both environmental and social conditions and the efficacy of policy strategies. Responses will involve reiteration of the problems and the response, and unless such reiterative capacity is designed into institutional and policy systems, *ad hocery* is the likely result. The persistence and flexibility of policy processes – and thus of the institutional systems in which they take place – are thus critical considerations in developing proposals for reform.

While these are general principles, they are practical in that careful consideration and implementation of them will render policy and institutional change more likely to be effective in the long term (if more complicated in the short term). If the above principles restate principles and arguments presented elsewhere in this book, that is perhaps confirmation of their importance and the pervasiveness of the challenge of evolving adaptive policy and institutions, rather than redundancy. They can be operationalised in various contexts via implementation of the policy and institutional options identified in this and some earlier chapters – whether they will or not, and whether such policy and institutional changes will be persisted with is another question, a brief reflection on which follows.

Concluding comment: prospects for environmental and sustainability policy

What are the prospects for embedding environment and sustainability into the policy and institutional landscape as central and routine concerns? Among those who have thought seriously about the task, some are deeply pessimistic, others guardedly optimistic. To end this discussion, we can consider the question of what would constitute a "credible commitment" to sustainability on the part of a jurisdiction and government, not in terms of absolute achievement but rather believable reforms which although incremental address the sustainability challenge in a purposeful manner:[7]

- The presence of a comprehensive, *integrated policy* platform on sustainable development, translating the general avowal of intent into operational policy principles and a plan of implementation, with sufficient resources and ongoing evaluation. Coordination of subsidiary policies and maintenance of social and policy debate around sustainability are less likely in the absence of framework policies at the meta- and macro-problem levels.

- Mandatory mechanisms to ensure *consideration of longer-term ecological and social issues* in policy-making, including specification of long-term information needs, statutory mandates for longevity and persistence of efforts, and provisions for ongoing review, evaluation and evolution of the policy response.

- Reform of the organisation of government to allow *whole-of-government approaches* to sustainability, with sufficient influence over traditional sectoral- and portfolio-specific agencies and imperatives to effect actual policy change.

- Implementation of *policy integration mechanisms* to enforce transparent incorporation of sustainability principles in all policy sectors and agencies, via procedures such as strategic environmental or sustainability assessment.

- Processes to identify and implement necessary changes to the wider body of *statute law*, to embed sustainability in the objects and processes of all public agencies and policy processes. This would be preceded by a wide-ranging legislative review to identify barriers to and opportunities for promoting sustainability in policy-making.

- Where necessary, and especially in federal systems, substantial renegotiation and reform of *intergovernmental policy and statutory arrangements* to allow more coordinated and effective responses to sustainability problems, including

---

7   The idea of a credible institutional commitment is loosely adapted from
     North (1993).

transfer of responsibilities and matching resources to the most suitable scale (subsidiarity).

- *Inclusion of the broader community* in policy processes, and encouragement and empowerment of community-based management approaches, including guarantees of ongoing capacity and support, and the transfer, where appropriate, of legal competence and decision-making power. An inclusive, higher-level body with defined roles (for example, NCSD) would be part of this participatory strategy.

- For developed countries, reform of *development aid and trade policy* to prioritise sustainability, and renewed commitment to, and planned implementation of, at minimum, the 0.7 per cent of GDP target for aid.

The mere existence of mechanisms such as the examples above is only part of the challenge, as is it the descriptors of "firm implementation", "mandatory", "independent evaluation" and "influence over other sectors" that will determine the quality of the institutional response in the longer term. It is certainly the case that no jurisdiction anywhere in the world could be ranked highly against all these and be able to boast such a commitment to policy and institutional change for sustainability. But if sustainability is a generational challenge, then realistically the above criteria set a high bar. There are many positive developments and achievements, scattered across sectors and jurisdictions. If we accept the long-term nature of the task, the size of the challenge and the uncertainty over which specific strategies will work best in a given context, then perhaps the hesitant and partial achievements to date are understandable and promising. A positive yet humble reading of sustainability and of progress to date recognises that things can indeed be done as well as how difficult it will be. This book has indicated that a great many options for policy and institutional change are available that address the challenges of environment and sustainability, all valid for different purposes and contexts. Amidst this complexity, there are strategies available that will suit both the longer- and shorter-term needs and possibilities for a specific policy-making situation.

It is arguably the case that the precise choice of strategy, assuming there are good grounds for the choice, will be less critical in the long run than persisting, testing and improving the response over time. Doing that in turn depends on the evolution of the policy domain of environment and sustainability into a more connected, informed and integrated arena of theory and practice than it is at present, bringing policy knowledge and capacity together with a sophisticated understanding of the nature of the problems in the domain. That is a big, long-term endeavour. Making a small contribution to that endeavour has been the aim of this book.

BIBLIOGRAPHY

Arnstein, S, 1969, A ladder of citizen participation, *Journal of the American Institute of Planners*, 35:216-224.

Attfield, R, 2003, Environmental Ethics: An Overview for the Twenty-First Century, Cambridge: Polity Press.

Baron, S, Field, J and Schuller, T, (eds), 2000, *Social Capital: Critical Perspectives*, Oxford: Oxford University Press.

Becker, E and Jahn, T, (eds), 1999, Sustainability and the Social Sciences: a Cross-disciplinary Approach to Integrating Environmental Considerations into Theoretical Reorientation, London: Zed Books.

Barnett, J, Ellemor, H and Dovers, S, 2003, Interdisciplinarity and sustainability, In: Dovers, S, Stern, D and Young, M, (eds), *New Dimensions in Ecological Economics: Integrated Approaches to People and Nature*, Cheltenham: Edward Elgar.

Bennett, CJ and Howlett, M, 1992, The lessons of learning: reconciling theories of policy learning and policy change, *Policy Sciences*, 25: 275–294.

Berkhout, F, Leach, M and Scoones, I, (eds), 2002, *Negotiating Environmental Change: New Perspectives from the Social Sciences*, Cheltenham: Edward Elgar.

Botkin, DB and Keller, EA, 2004, *Environmental Science: Earth as a Living Planet*, 5th edn, New York: Wiley.

Boulding, K, 1966, The economics of coming spaceship Earth, In: Jarratt, H, (ed), *Environmental Quality in a Growing Economy*, Baltimore: Johns Hopkins University Press.

Boyden, SV, 1987, Western Civilization in Biological Perspective: Patterns in Biohistory, Oxford: Clarendon Press.

Bridgman, P and Davis, G, 2001, *The Australian Policy Handbook*, Sydney: Allen & Unwin.

Brooks, S and Gagnon, A-G, (eds), 1990, *Social Scientists, Policy, and the State*, New York: Praeger.

Brunner, RD, 1991, The policy movement as policy problem, *Policy Sciences*, 24: 65–98.

Brunner, RD, 1996, A milestone in the policy sciences, *Policy Sciences*, 29: 45–68.

Carley, M and Christie, M, 2000, *Managing Sustainable Development*, 2nd edn, London: Earthscan.

Chasek, PS, (ed), 2000, The Global Environment in the Twenty-First Century: Prospects For International Cooperation, Tokyo: United Nations University Press.

Christensen, T and Lægreid, P, (eds), 2002, New Public Management: the Transformation of Ideas and Practice, Hampshire: Ashgate.

Colebatch, H, 1998, *Policy*, Buckingham: Open University Press.

Common, M, 1995, *Sustainability and Policy: Limits to Economics*, Melbourne: Cambridge University Press.

Common, M, 2003, Economics, In: Page, E and Proops, J, (eds), *Environmental Thought*, Cheltenham: Edward Elgar.

Connor, R and Dovers, S, 2004, *Institutional Change for Sustainable Development,* Cheltenham: Edward Elgar.

Cranor, CF, 1999, Asymmetric information, the precautionary principle, and burdens of proof, In: Raffensperger, C and Tickner, J, (eds), *Protecting Public Health and the Environment: Implementing the Precautionary Principle,* Washington DC: Island Press.

Daneke, GA, 1989, On paradigmatic progress in public policy and administration, *Policy Studies Journal,* 17: 275–296.

Davis, G, 1993, Introduction: public policy in the 1990s, In: Hede, A and Prasser, S, (eds), *Policy-making in Volatile Times,* pp,15–26, Sydney: Hale & Iremonger.

Davis, G, Wanna, J, Warhurst, J and Weller, P, 1993, *Public Policy in Australia,* Sydney: Allen & Unwin.

Dery, D, 1984, *Problem Definition in Policy Analysis,* Lawrence: University of Kansas Press.

Dobson, A, 2003, *Citizenship and the Environment,* Oxford: Oxford University Press.

Dolšak, N and Ostrom, E, (eds), 2003, *The Commons in the New Millennium: Challenges and Adaptations,* Cambridge MA: MIT Press.

Dovers, S, 1995, A framework for scaling and framing policy problems in sustainability, *Ecological Economics,* 12: 93–106.

Dovers, 1997, Sustainability: demands on policy, *Journal of Public Policy,* 16: 303–318.

Dovers, S, 2001, Informing policy and institutions, In: Venning, J and Higgins, J, (eds), *Towards Sustainability: Emerging Systems for Informing Sustainable Development,* Sydney: University of NSW Press.

Dovers, S, 2002, Too deep a SEA? Strategic environmental assessment in the era of sustainability, In: Marsden, S and Dovers, S, (eds), *Strategic Environmental Assessment in Australasia,* Sydney: Federation Press.

Dovers, S, 2003, A policy orientation as integrative strategy, In: Dovers, S, Stern, D and Young, M, (eds), *New Dimensions in Ecological Economics: Integrated Approaches to People and Nature,* Cheltenham: Edward Elgar.

Dovers, S and Handmer, J, 1995, Ignorance, the precautionary principle, and sustainability, *Ambio,* 24: 92–97.

Dovers, S and Mobbs, C, 1997, An alluring prospect? Ecology, and the requirements of adaptive management, In: Klomp, N and Lunt, N, (eds), *Frontiers in Ecology: Building the Links,* London: Elsevier.

Dovers, S and Wild River, S, 2003, *Managing Australia's Environment,* Sydney: Federation Press.

Dryzek, J, 1997, *The Politics of the Earth: Environmental Discourses,* Oxford: Oxford University Press.

Dryzek, J, 2000, Deliberative Democracy and Beyond: Liberals, Critics, Contestations, Oxford: Oxford University Press.

Dye, TR, 1983, *Understanding Public Policy,* Englewood Cliffs, NJ: Prentice-Hall.

Elliott, L, 2004, *Global Politics of the Environment,* 2nd edn, Hampshire: Palgrave Macmillan.

Elster, J, (ed), 1998, *Deliberative Democracy,* Cambridge: Cambridge University Press.

Etzioni, A, 1967, Mixed scanning: a third approach to decision-making, *Public Administration Review,* 27: 385–392.

Finer, SE, 1997, *The History of Government from the Earliest Times*, Oxford: Oxford University Press.

Fischer, F, 2003, Reframing Public Policy: Discursive Politics and Deliberative Practices, Oxford: Oxford University Press.

Fung, A and Wright, EO, (eds), 2003, Deepening Democracy: Institutional Innovation in Empowered Participatory Governance, London: Verso.

Funtowicz, S and Ravetz, J, 1991, A new scientific methodology for global environmental issues, In: Costanza, R, (ed), *Ecological Economics: The Science and Management of Sustainability*, New York: Columbia University Press.

Garrod, G and Willis, K, 1999, Economic Valuation of the Environment: Methods and Case Studies, Cheltenham: Edward Elgar.

Garson, GD, 1986, From policy science to policy analysis: a quarter century of progress, In: Dunn, WN, (ed), *Policy Analysis: Perspectives, Concepts and Methods*, Greenwich, Conn: JAI Press.

Gibson, RB, Hassan, S, Holtz, S, Tansey, J and Whitelaw, G, 2005, *Sustainability Assessment: Criteria, Processes and Applications*, London: Earthscan.

Gillroy, JM and Wade, M, (eds), 1992, *The Moral Dimensions of Public Policy Choice: Beyond the Market Paradigm*, Pittsburgh: University of Pittsburgh Press.

Goodin, RE, 1996, Institutions and their design, In: Goodin, RE, (ed), *The Theory of Institutional Design*, Cambridge: Cambridge University Press.

Gunderson, LH, Holling, CS and Light, SS, (eds), 1995, *Barriers and Bridges to the Renewal of Ecosystems and Institutions*, New York: Columbia University Press.

Gunningham, N and Grabosky, P, 1998, *Smart Regulation: Designing Environmental Policy*, Oxford: Clarendon Press.

Hajer, M and Wagenaar, H, (eds), 2003, Deliberative Policy Analysis: Understanding Governance in the Network Society, Cambridge: Cambridge University Press.

Handmer, J and Dovers, S, 1996, A typology of resilience: rethinking institutions for sustainability, *Industrial and Environmental Crisis Quarterly*, 9: 482–511.

Harris, F, (ed), 2004, *Global Environmental Issues*, Hoboken NJ: Wiley.

Harrison, P, 1992, The Third Revolution: Population, Environment, and a Sustainable World, Harmondsworth: Penguin.

Healey, P, 1997, Collaborative Planning: Shaping Places in Fragmented Societies, London: Macmillan.

Hogwood, BW and Gunn, LA, 1984, *Policy Analysis for the Real World*, Oxford: Oxford University Press.

Holling, CS, (ed), 1978, Adaptive Environmental Management and Assessment, Chichester: Wiley.

Hood, C, 1986, *The Tools of Government*, Chatham NJ: Chatham House.

Horowitz, IL and Katz, JE, 1975, *Social Science and Public Policy in the United States*, New York: Praeger.

Howlett, M, 1991, Policy instruments, policy styles, and policy implementation: national approaches to theories of instrument choice, *Policy Studies Journal*, 19: 1–21.

Howlett, M and Ramesh, M, 2003, *Studying Public Policy: Policy Cycles and Policy Subsystems*, Don Mills, Ontario: Oxford University Press.

Jakeman, AJ and Letcher, RA, Integrated assessment and modelling: features, principles and examples for catchment management, *Environmental Modelling and Software*, 18: 491–501.

Jenkins-Smith, H and Sabatier, P, 1994, Evaluating the advocacy coalition framework, *Journal of Public Policy*, 14: 175–203.

Kingdon, JW, 1984, *Agendas, Alternatives and Public Policy*, Boston: Little, Brown.

Lafferty, WM, (ed), 2004, Governance for Sustainable Development: the Challenge of Adapting Form to Function, Cheltenham: Edward Elgar.

Lafferty, WM and Meadowcroft, J, (eds), 2000, *Implementing Sustainable Development*, Oxford: Oxford University Press.

Lasswell, H, 1951, The policy orientation, In: Lerner, D and Lasswell, H, (eds), *The Policy Sciences: Recent Developments in Scope and Methods*, Stanford: Stanford University Press.

Lasswell, H, 1971, *A Pre-view of the Policy Sciences*, New York: Elsevier.

Lee, KN, 1993, Compass and Gyroscope: Integrating Science and Politics for the Environment, Washington: Island Press.

Leeuw, FL, Rist, RC and Sonnichsen, RC, (eds), 1994, *Can Governments Learn? Comparative Perspectives on Evaluation and Organizational Learning*, New Brunswick NJ: Transaction Publishers.

Lenschow, A, (ed), 2002, *Environmental Policy Integration*, London: Earthscan.

Lindblom, CE, 1959, The science of muddling through, *Public Administration Review*, 19: 79–88.

Lindblom, CE, 1979, Still muddling, not yet through, *Public Administration Review*, 39: 517–526.

Lindblom, CE and Cohen, DK, 1979, *Usable Knowledge: Social Science and Social Problem Solving*, New Haven: Yale University Press.

Linder, SH and Peters, BG, 1989, Instruments of government: perceptions and contexts, *Journal of Public Policy*, 9: 35–58.

Machiavelli, N, 1940 (1532), *The Prince*, New York: Random House.

March, JG and Olsen, JP, 1979, *Ambiguity and Choice in Organizations*, Bergen: Universitetsforlaget.

Marsden, S and Dovers, S, (eds), 2002, *Strategic Environmental Assessment in Australasia*, Sydney: Federation Press.

May, P, 1992, Policy learning and policy failure, *Journal of Public Policy*, 12: 331–354.

McLaughlin, K, Osborne, SP and Ferlie, E, (eds), 2002, *New Public Management: current trends and future prospects*, London: Routledge.

McNeill, JR, 2001, Something New Under the Sun: An Environmental History of the Twentieth Century, London: Penguin.

Meadows, DH, Meadows, DL, Randers, J and Behrens, WW, 1972, *Limits to Growth: A Report for the Club of Rome's Project on the Predicament of Mankind*, New York: Universal Books.

Munton, R, 2003, Deliberative democracy and environmental decision-making, In: Berkhout, F, Leach, M and Scoones, I, (eds), *Negotiating Environmental Change: New Perspectives from the Social Sciences*, Cheltenham: Edward Elgar.

North, DC, 1990, Institutions, Institutional Change and Economic Performance, Cambridge: Cambridge University Press.

North, DC, 1993, Institutions and Credible Commitment, *Journal of Institutional and Theoretical Economics*, 149(1): 11–28.

OECD (Organization for Economic Cooperation and Development), Various years, *Performance Reviews* (various countries), Paris: OECD.

Ostrom, E, 1990, Governing the Commons: The Evolution of Institutions for Collective Action, Cambridge MA: Cambridge University Press.

Paehlke, R and Torgerson, D, 1990, Managing Leviathan: Environmental Politics and the Administrative State, London: Belhaven Press.

Page, E and Proops, J, (eds) 2003, *Environmental Thought*, Cheltenham: Edward Elgar.

Partidario, M and Clark, R, (eds), *Perspectives on Strategic Environmental Assessment*, Boca Raton: CRC Lewis Publishers.

Patton, MQ, 1997, Utilisation-focused Evaluation: the New Century Text, Thousand Oaks CL: Sage.

Pellikaan, H and Van Der Veen, RJ, 2002, *Environmental Dilemmas and Policy Design*, Cambridge: Cambridge University Press.

Peters, BG and Pierre, J, 2003, *Handbook of Public Administration*, London: Sage.

Ponting, C, 1990, *A Green History of the World*, Harmondsworth: Penguin.

Putnam, RD, 2000, Bowling Alone: The Collapse and Revival of American Community, New York: Simon and Schuster.

Renn, O, Webler, T and Wiedermann, P, (eds), 1995, Fairness and Competence in Citizen Participation: Evaluating Models for Environmental Discourse, Dordrecht: Kluwer.

Rose, R, 2005, Learning from Comparative Public Policy: A Practical Guide London: Routledge.

Smithson, M, 1989, *Ignorance and Uncertainty: Emerging Paradigms*, New York: Springer-Verlag.

Speth, G, (ed), 2003, *Worlds Apart: Globalization and the Environment*, Washington DC: Island Press.

Sterner, T, 2002, Policy Instruments for Environmental and Natural Resource Management, Washington DC: Resources for the Future Press.

Stewart, J and Jones, G, 2003, *Renegotiating the Environment: The Power of Politics*, Sydney: Federation Press.

Stokke, OS and Thommessen, ØB, (eds), 2001, Yearbook of International Co-operation on Environment and Development, 2001/2002, London: Earthscan.

Swanson, D, Pinter, I, Bregha, L, Volkery, A and Jacob, K, 2004, *National Strategies for Sustainable Development*, Winnipeg: International Institute for Sustainable Development.

Torgerson, D, 1986, Between knowledge and politics: three faces of policy analysis, *Policy Sciences*, 19: 33–59.

UN (United Nations,) 1992, *Agenda 21: The UN Programme of Action from Rio*, New York: United Nations.

Venning, J and Higgins, J, (eds), 2001, Towards Sustainability: Emerging Systems for Informing Sustainable Development, Sydney: University of NSW Press.

Walker, KJ, 1992, Conclusion: the politics of environmental policy, In: Walker, KJ, (ed), *Australian Environmental Policy: Ten Case Studies*, Sydney: University of NSW Press.

Wilson, EO, 1994, *The Diversity of Life*, Harmondsworth: Penguin.

WCED (World Commission on Environment and Development), 1987, *Our Common Future*, Oxford: Oxford University Press.

Wynne, B, 1992, Uncertainty and environmental learning: reconceiving science in the preventative paradigm, *Global Environmental Change*, 2: 111–127.

INDEX

policy monitoring and evaluation,
in, 137-141
categories of, 139
levels of detail, 140
policy processes, in, 28-29
political learning, 29
social learning, 29
Policy models
policy cycles, of *see* Policy cycle
policy processes, of *see* Policy
processes
preconditions, 58
utility of, 26
Policy network
responsibilities of, 13
use of term, 14
Policy principles
environment and sustainability
policy, for, 93-98
benefits, 93-94
sources, 94
precautionary principle, 82, 85-86,
172-173
Policy problems
considerations, 41-42
issues distinguished from, 41-50
policy processes
problem-framing stage in *see*
Policy processes
responses to, 52-54
community involvement, 52
environmental policy
instruments, 52
government policy, 52
international policies and
agreements, 52
market mechanisms, use of, 52
mega-departments, development
of, 53
multi-stakeholder partnerships,
53
substantive issues, 41
sustainability, 41-50
assets, non-traded and non-
valued, 47
community involvement, need
for, 48
complexity and connectivity, 45-
46
costs and benefits, public and
private, 47-48
cumulative impacts, 45

ecological limits and
thresholds, 45
ill-defined rights and
responsibilities, 47
irreversible impacts, 45
key attributes, 43-50
lack of research methods, 47
moral concerns, 46
novelty, 48
policy and institutional
challenges, 50-51
poor information, 46
research, integrative/
interdisciplinary, 49
risk, 46
spatial and temporal scale, 44
systemic causes, 46
uncertainty, 46
Policy processes
enduring questions in, 24-30
authority and decision-making,
27-28
incrementalism, 25, 55
"policy analysis as
handmaiden", 24
policy instrument choice, 28
policy learning, 28-29
politics, values and the state,
26-27
problem definition, 27
rational-comprehensive
approach, 25, 55
rational or non-rational policy,
25-26
role and use of information,
29-30
explanation of, 6, 12
issues, identification and
discussion of, 43
models of, 26, 56
accountability, 66
analysis, of, 67
checklist, 66-67
communication, 66
description of, 67
general elements, 65-66
knowledge, 67-70
policy co-ordination and
integration, 66
prescription, 67
public participation and
stakeholder involvement, 66
stages in, 59-65
transparency, 66